Heritage Gardens

Heirloom Seeds

Melded Cultures with a Pennsylvania German Accent

Michael B. Emery
& Irwin Richman

Schiffer Publishing Ltd
4880 Lower Valley Road • Atglen, PA 19310

Designed by Danielle D. Farmer
Cover design by Danielle D. Farmer
Type set in ChopinScript/GrutchGroteskShaded/GrutchGrotesk/Myriad Pro

On front cover, top: Illustration from *The Cottage Collection*. Bottom: Historic Schaefferstown.
Back cover, clockwise from top left: *The Cottage Collection*, LItitz Historical Museum, Landis Valley, and Landis Valley.

ISBN: 978-0-7643-4863-1
Printed in China

Published by Schiffer Publishing, Ltd.
4880 Lower Valley Road
Atglen, PA 19310
Phone: (610) 593-1777; Fax: (610) 593-2002
E-mail: Info@schifferbooks.com

For our complete selection of fine books on this and related subjects, please visit our website at www.schifferbooks.com. You may also write for a free catalog.

This book may be purchased from the publisher. Please try your bookstore first.

We are always looking for people to write books on new and related subjects. If you have an idea for a book, please contact us at proposals@schifferbooks.com.

Schiffer Publishing's titles are available at special discounts for bulk purchases for sales promotions or premiums. Special editions, including personalized covers, corporate imprints, and excerpts can be created in large quantities for special needs. For more information, contact the publisher.

DEDICATION

Mike dedicates this book to his parents, Logan and the late Ruth Ann Emery, to his wife Alia, who has been supportive (or at least tolerant) of his historical interests and his collecting habits, and to their children, Joshua and Nora. Irwin dedicates his work to his wife, Sue, who countenances and usually encourages his interests; their sons, Dr. Alexander Richman, a mathematician, and Dr. Joshua Richman, a medical researcher; their grandchildren, Benjamin and Zoë; and honorary son, Oscar Beisert, an architectural historian.

CONTENTS

Acknowledgments 6

I. Which Came First, the Garden or the Seed? 7

II. The Heritage Garden 17

III. Visiting Gardens, Garden Sites, and Heritage Landscapes 99

IV. Heirloom Seeds 185

V. The Galleries 237

    A Gallery of Heirloom Vegetables 238
    A Gallery of Heirloom Flowers and Herbs 250
    A Love for Exotics 264
    An Endnote 266

Appendix A: Heritage Garden Addresses and Contact Information 266
Appendix B: Heirloom Seed Sources 268

Sources and Suggestions for Additional Reading 269

Index 271

ACKNOWLEDGMENTS

Two very different people from very different backgrounds came together to write this book, their fourth collaboration. They are a generation and a half apart, but joined by stories of horseradish, among other life experiences. Mike's mother told him about her chores down on the farm, including the family's harvest of the pungent root. Irwin remembers his grandfather using a hand grinder on the horseradish in the summer kitchen of his house in New York's Catskill Mountains, pausing only to dry his tears.

Of special importance are our colleagues at the Landis Valley Village and Farm Museum, beginning with James Lewars, our always supportive museum director. Curators Bruce Bomberger and Jen Royer are experts on horticultural equipment within our collections. Joe Schott, our farm and garden manager, is an authority on historical agriculture and an expert fruit grafter. Beth Leensvart and Mickie Blefko of the Landis Valley Heirloom Seed Project have been helpful. Our other colleagues have always provided support when they could. Thank you Nicole Wagner, Tim Essig, Will Morrow, Joyce Perkinson, Jaime Schuring, Cindy Reedy, Shayla Larey, and Doris Tobias. Russell Eaton, a retired physicist who has cataloged the Landis Valley postcard collection, brought many items to our attention.

Of special note is Craig Benner of our sister institution, the Railroad Museum of Pennsylvania, and a fine professional photographer who did a number of the photographs for this book.

Many individuals and institutions helped us along the way and provided illustrations. Thank you all: Melanie Hady, York County Heritage Trust; Dianne Cram & Kimberly Boice, Peter Wentz Farmstead; Dade Royer, Renfrew Museum and Park; Melanie Gettier, Frederick County Landmarks Foundation; Kaytlin Sumner, Johnstown Area Heritage Association; Chris Owens, Historic Rittenhouse Town; Laura Keim, Stenton; Alice Oskam & Emily & Linda Holt, Historic Schaefferstown Inc.; Deborah DiPasquale, Quiet Valley Historical Living Farm; Kristin Hagar, Wyck Historic House, Garden, and Farm; Megan van Ravenswaay, Moravian Historical Society; Cory Van Brookhoven, Lititz Historical Foundation; Tom Wentzel, Lititz Moravian Church; Ellen Kutcher, Historic Bethabara Park; Ella Aderman & Linda S. Callegari, Pennypacker Mills; Gary Albert, Old Salem Museums & Gardens; Kim Massare, John Bartram Association; David Miller, Old Economy Village; Joy Woppert, Colonial Pennsylvania Plantation; Doug Miller & Tabitha Dardes, Pennsbury Manor; Kathryn Pannepacker, Grumblethorpe; Bonnie Murray & Julia Lo Ehrhardt, Mt. Cuba Center, Inc.; Susan J. Crane, Morris Arboretum of the University of Pennsylvania; Jacqueline Falco-Smith, Cedar Rapids Museum of Art; Anne Crouchley, Joslyn Art Museum; Christine Berube & Heidi J. McCausland, Johnny's Selected Seeds; Becky Gochnauer, 1719 Hans Herr House & Museum; Jan Musser Geier, Historic Bethlehem Museums & Sites; Jennifer Pennington, Bowman's Hill Wildflower Preserve; Justin Reiter, Frontier Culture Museum of Virginia; Kay Menick & Ann Miniutti, Art Resource; Susan I. Newton, Winterthur Museum; Riche Sorensen, Smithsonian American Art Museum; Stacey C. Peeples, Pennsylvania Hospital; Jennifer Lanman, Swope Art Museum; Lucie Amour, VAGA.

Mike is computer literate, while Irwin is not. Special thanks go to Irwin's wife, Dr. M. Susan Richman, retired mathematician and university dean, for turning Irwin's scrawl into usable text and for her valued editing help.

I.

Which Came First,

the Garden or the Seed?

BEAUDETTE, MINN

Copyrighted Photograph 1908
by W. H. Martin

Here is the place we grow large cabbage

The dream of the heritage farmer or gardener is a picture-perfect harvest or even a fantastic one!
Cabbage: The Cottage Collection

An appreciation for locally sourced foodstuffs is snowballing in contemporary America. The locavore movement is strong and growing. "Locavore" was coined in 2005 by chef and food writer Jessica Prentice, as an identifier for an emerging mantra: eat local. Ideally, "local" means food grown in your own community but, practically, locavores talk about food coming from a "food shed." Most locavores define local as any foodstuff within a 100- or up to a 250-mile radius of the consumption point. Most locavores make exceptions for spices, coffee, and tea, but always try to deal with small purveyors or, in the case of coffee, small roasters. Ideally, you should know your supplier. Accordingly, today even supermarkets feature local produce, from identified sources.

In reading the menu in a trendy metropolitan restaurant today, the traditional mass-marketing description is not good enough. A "Tomato and Lettuce Salad" is unheard of. Even a "Luscious Seasonal Tomato and Lettuce Salad" is suspect. We expect nothing less than "A Salad of Heirloom Tomatoes grown on our countryside farm, resting on a bed of baby lettuces from [*insert appropriate name*] growers right here in [*insert your town or city*], dressed with a vinaigrette of herbs raised on our rooftop herb garden."

It may be an extreme claim, but in the twenty-first century, for many Americans the pursuit of fresh, pure, local foods has become a major religious-like movement, complete with its own pilgrimages. Blue Hill at Stone Barns Restaurant is, for locavores, the modern Jerusalem or Mecca. On a portion of the former Rockefeller estate at Pocantico Hills, New York, Blue Hill sources many of its foods in sight of the diners. As the restaurant owners note: "There are no menus … instead, the restaurant offers multi-course farmers' feasts based on the day's harvest,"—including bounty from the vast greenhouses. Dinner in 2015: "Grazing, Peeking, Rooting," is $198 per person. The best in locavore fare comes at a price.

Locavore inclinations often lead to an appreciation of heirloom vegetables and fruits, which are often distinctively flavored, especially when consumed at their peak of freshness. Proclaim the glories of heirloom fruits and vegetables and historic livestock. Besides, what could be better for the psyche than antique plant varieties—those developed before modern chemical-drenched, genetically altered agriculture. As ancillaries, why not heirloom herbs and flowers?

Arguably, the historic value of heirloom plants was appreciated before their gastronomic virtues. All of this is thanks to the multiplication of historic house museums and outdoor or farm museums. At first it was enough to keep the grass cut and the gardens neat. Then questions were asked—is the garden style appropriate to the house? What is the appropriate form? Once the question of style or form was answered, the next question became, "Are the plant varieties accurate?" A resounding "No" led to the conscious establishment of a heritage seed program that could piggyback on the work of even earlier hobbyists and scholars who collected antique varieties of esculents, fruits, and vegetables to preserve them from extinction or to recapture ancestral treasures.

For example, Frank Weier of Vineland, Ontario, Canada, a Russian Mennonite, writes about his quest for seeds his family knew. "My parents," he notes, "left Russia in 1926 and due to political circumstances were not able to bring many possessions with them." What Frank wants to find are, "… any seeds from Russia, preferably with a Mennonite background."

Unblemished produce allows for the creation of picture-perfect healthful food.

In a 1987 letter written to Lee Stoltzfus, a founder of the Heirloom Seed Project of the Landis Valley Village and Farm Museum in Lancaster, Pennsylvania, Hayward Barnett of Missouri writes about his beans:

I am happy to share my Russian Mennonite seeds with you and am happy to see that they are going into a restored Mennonite garden.

These bean seeds came to me in 1984 from a Mr. Ralph Warner, 1958 E. Lark, Springfield, Mo., who got them from his son-in-law, Lyle Frosese. These beans are said to have been in the family since the Mennonite ancestors came to Kansas from Germany in the 1870s and who had fled Russia to Germany.

Mr. Warner said to pick the beans as usual when they are mature. String them while green and snap them as usual. Then let them dry in the pod. When dry, store in a mesh bag. To cook, wash the beans at least once then cook until done. I do not really understand the purpose for all of this. I tried it one time and wasn't sure if I was doing it right and didn't see that I was accomplishing much so I have never tried it again. I don't know if this is from an old Mennonite custom or not, maybe you will know.

The seeds were also shared with Frank in Ontario.

John E. Withee (1910–1993), a Maine native, had a romance with beans that went back into the 1930s when he learned how to bake enough beans in a cast-iron pot in a pit or "beanhole" for twenty-four hours to feed hundreds of people at one sitting. Fast forward to 1970 when he decided to "throw a bean-hole bash for a few dozen people" at his Massachusetts home. Past experience taught him that Jacob's Cattle beans were best for his event, but he couldn't find any of the medium size, slender white bean, splashed with maroon. His second choice was a similar bean, Soldier, also a white marked with red, but they were also unavailable, so he settled for ubiquitous, general purpose navy beans.

Afterwards he began his quest for Jacob's Cattle, finally finding a few pounds of seeds in a country store in Keene, New Hampshire. Sharing the story of the quest with his relatives in Maine, he "... figured if that one was hard to find, what must be happening to some of the other varieties?" He now was a dedicated saver of heirloom beans. His Maine relatives spread the word and over the next six years he accumulated more than 100 varieties that he stored in an odd assortment of "... matchboxes, plastic bread bags [and] discarded paper cups" in a cool, dark closet. Because bean seeds lose viability after five years, every year he grew a few seeds in his garden to maintain viability.

Retiring as a medical photographer at a Boston hospital in 1976, he turned to his beans with a passion fueled by available time. By 1981 he was growing 230 varieties of beans!

Ideally the garden is a place of serene beauty as exemplified by *A Lady Picking Peonies* by William Verplanck Birnery (1858–1909). *Private collection.*

The ideal garden is weed-free, and its rows straight. The ideal harvester is sweat-free and in nostalgic costume.

You can have a good time here I know. I've tried it.

To help him with his beans, he founded a nonprofit called Wanigan Associates. "Wanigan" is derived from an Abnaki Indian word meaning " that into one strays." The organization would eventually donate its collections to Seed Savers Exchange in Princeton, Missouri, and the Organic Gardening and Research Center in Kutztown, Pennsylvania. Withee, freed of his curatorial responsibilities, could devote himself to becoming a premier expert and writer about beans.

Much younger than Withee, Guy Thomas came to beans when looking for a crop to grow on a farm he had bought in Castleton, Vermont. In 1975 he tried beans and results were poor because of a very wet fall. He did learn that there wasn't one seed merchant in the US who offered a significant selection of bean seeds. And an idea was formed that led to the Vermont Bean Seed Company, which, by 1982, was offering seventy-two varieties. The company offers more today, along with other vegetable seeds and plants, not all antique.

The bean story can be replicated with examples drawn from lovers of apples, mushrooms, lettuce, melons, and tomatoes ... some of whom you'll meet later in the book. Which came first—an appreciation of the historically correct or heritage garden or the heirloom seed? The heritage garden wins hands down. Which has been the most widely influential? The heirloom seed. Demand for yesterday's varieties keeps growing. Let us explore gardens first.

In reality, not all gardening is pleasurable and many heritage gardeners are put off by
the impersonal industrial scale of contemporary vegetable production.

Top left | Heirloom plants can have historic origins. What is more familiar than a geranium (*Pelargonium*) growing as a potted plant in a farmhouse window, started from a slip given by a mother, a grandmother, an aunt, or a friend—the very definition of an heirloom plant. One of the first geranium plants introduced into America from Africa via Europe is proudly displayed by artist-botanist Rubens Peale (1784–1865) and recorded by his brother Raphaelle (1774–1825). *The National Gallery of Art.*

Top right | The transmission of culture is symbolized by a plant held by a pioneer woman of Iowa. Against the background of a beautiful landscape she helped shape, a proud hardworking woman displays a sturdy, but purely ornamental snake plant (*sansevieria trifasciata*), immortalized by American Regionalist artist Grant Woods (1891–1942). *Cedar Rapids Museum of Art.*

The Flower Girl, painted by Charles C. Ingham (1796–1863) in 1846, portrays a range of garden flowers and exotics available by the mid-nineteenth century. Contemporary at that time, these varieties are heirlooms today. *The Metropolitan Museum of Art, gift of William Church Osborn.*

To look at nineteenth-century American still-life paintings is to look at a veritable catalog of what are now considered to be heirloom plants. Central to the development of the still-life tradition in America are members of the Peale dynasty, painters of Philadelphia. Raphaelle Peale's *Melons and Morning Glories* (top) and his uncle James Peale's (1749–1831) *Vegetable with Yellow Blossoms* (bottom left) and *Still Life with Balsam Apple* (bottom right), are especially luscious and ultimately informative. *"Morning Glories," National Museum of American Art, The Smithsonian Institution; "Vegetables," The Henry Francis du Pont Winterthur Museum; "Balsam Apple," The Metropolitan Museum of Art.*

II.

The Heritage Garden

The garden is an indelible element of the ideal American landscape. This has never been portrayed more lyrically than in *Stone City, Iowa*, by Grant Wood, painted in 1930. *Joslyn Art Museum, Omaha, Nebraska.*

The garden is as ordered and American as the quilts on the clothesline and the iris lined up like well-disciplined troops in Grant Wood's 1941 homage to the small-town Midwest, *Spring in Town. The Sheldon Swope Art Museum, Terre Haute, Indiana*

The study of garden history is exhaustive and varied. Gardens as exotic as those of ancient Egypt and the Chinese Han Dynasty have been shown to have influenced Western garden tradition. Historically, attention has been given to high-style gardens, the gardens of the rich and powerful, and especially to the pleasure and display gardens. Increasingly, more attention is given to the gardens of everyday life and folk gardens, whose forms are often influenced by archaic high style or lost in the mists of time.

America's heritage gardens are reflective of the peoples who populated our North American landmass. When the Europeans arrived in the New World they discovered new crops. Generations of school children past learned about the Indians teaching the Pilgrims how to grow corn, pumpkins and squash, and beans ("The Three Sisters"), which helped the colonists survive.

To dig in the earth is manly. For kids to stand in for adults is clearly adorable. *"Bulk Seeds,"* Collection of Mr. and Mrs. Michael B. Emery. Others, The Cottage Collection.

Easter symbolizes the beginning of a growing season. A fruit tree blooms. Eggs promise emerging life. A lamb is at the beginning of life. At Thanksgiving the harvest is proclaimed. Crops are mature and the tom turkey is at his prime. *The Cottage Collection*.

A man is photographed on a hillside overlooking the carefully cultivated back lots of houses in Bernville, Berks County, in Pennsylvania Dutch Country, circa 1885 by photographer C. G. Blatt. *Collection of the late Lester Breininger*.

When growing areas are too big for humans to cultivate, animal power is called in. Oxen plow a field in Upper Canada Village, Ontario. *The Cottage Collection*.

Posing for photographs in and near gardens is a natural. Clockwise from top left: Hat-bedecked Pearl McClure of Oak Park, Illinois, stands next to a dazzling floral display; "The Stuckey Family" pose on and near a sloped garden patch, probably in western Pennsylvania; Anette Barre of North Adams, Massachusetts proudly notes that, "This is me in one of our flower beds … it looks beautiful,"; and four young Lancaster County, Pennsylvania, women and a dog stand in front of a garden fence. *The Cottage Collection.*

Rote   LANCASTER, PA.

Kraus   Electric Light   Harrisburg.
              Studio.

Women in studios were often photographed amidst garden-oriented props and backgrounds. *The Cottage Collection.*

NATIVE AMERICAN GARDENS

When the Spanish conquered Peru and Mexico in the sixteenth century they discovered very elaborate gardens, both vegetable and flower. Most Native American gardening was less impressive. However, virtually all early travelers in America made mention of the vegetables the Indians grew. Native American agriculture was hampered by a lack of any beasts of burden; the only domesticated animal was the dog. Most farming and gardening was carried out by squaws, whom the explorer Samuel de Champlain derisively called "the Indian's mule."

Early travelers credited the Cherokees, then living in Georgia and Carolina, as the best gardeners in the American southeast. They grew marsh mallow, *Althaea officinalis*, for its mucilaginous root, along with sunflowers, squash, gourds, beans and, of course, corn, which the Europeans all adopted. Thomas Ash, writing in the seventeenth century about residents of Charles Town, South Carolina, noted in *Carolina, or a Description of the Present State of That Country, etc.*:

Their Provision which grows in the Field is chiefly Indian Corn, which produces a vast Increase, yearly, yielding Two plentiful Harvests, of which they make a wholesome Bread, and good Biskit, which give a strong, sound, and nourishing Diet; with Milk I have eaten it dress'd in various ways: Of the Juice of the Corn, when green, the Spaniards with chocolet, aromatis'd with Spices, make a rare Drink of an excellent Delicacy. I have seen the English among the Caribbes roast the green Ear on the Coals, and eat it with a great deal of Pleasure. The Indians in Carolina parch the ripe Corn, then pound it to a Powder, putting it in a Leathern Bag: When they use it they take a little quantity of the Powder in the Palm of their Hands, mixing it with Water, and sup it off: with this they will travel for several days. . . The American Physicians observe that it breeds good Blood, removes and opens Oppellation and Obstructions. At Carolina they lately invented a way of making with it a good sound Beer; but it's strong and heady: By Maceration, when duly fermented, a strong Spirit like Brandy may be drawn off from it, by the help of an Alembic [a still].

In the northeast, the Iroquois were especially known for their agriculture. The Senecas of New York, an allied people, grew more than a dozen varieties of corn, which they carefully cultivated "... even understanding that varieties planted too close together would 'visit' and establish 'colonies' on the cobs of their neighbors," as U. P. Hedrick noted in *A History of Horticulture in America to 1860*. Growing sunflower seeds for oil, along with squashes and melons, they also ate a variety of wild foods, including what we now call Jerusalem artichoke or sunchoke (*Helianthus tuberosus*) tubers, which we now cultivate.

Native to the Indian gardens of North America were four species of bean belonging to the genus *Phaseolus*, each with many varieties. Most common were varieties of *Phaseolus vulgaris* including common pole and bush beans. Next are *Phaseolus lunatus* or lima beans, and *Phaseolus coccineuw*, the red blooming scarlet runner bean. In the arid regions of Arizona and New Mexico *Phaseolus acutifolius*, the tepary bean, was extremely important.

Native Americans were our first gardeners and their agriculture interested early explorers. John White (1540–1593) recorded, "Indian gardens on Roanoke Island" in North Carolina in 1586. He also detailed "Indians planting corn and beans." Corn was the most important grain the New World gave the Old. The illustrations are from Theodore de Bry's *India Occidentalis, 1590–1591, The Library of Congress.*

Tobacco (*Nicotiana*), a Native American crop, would dramatically affect the human condition. It was commonly smoked by Indians. The vignette is from the sixteenth century. *Tobacco, The Cottage Collection; The Library of Congress.*

Collecting the Sap of the SUGAR MAPLE

Mankind has a sweet tooth and any addition to the sweetness larder was welcome. The Native Americans introduced maple sugar to the settlers, who developed the techniques. Maple sugaring became emblematic of New England, although it is practiced wherever the sugar maple (*Acer saccharium*) thrives. *The Cottage Collection.*

Native Americans prized wild mushrooms, but they didn't understand their culture. The Morel (*Morchella esculenta*), highly prized today, still can not be cultivated. *The Cottage Collection.*

The Jerusalem artichoke (*Helianthus tuberosus*) is another native plant that American Indians cultivated. A member of the sunflower family, the tubers are known by many names. As "sun chokes" they are popular with contemporary "foodies." *Photograph, Lee Stoltzfus; engraving, Johnson and Stokes Catalog, 1898.*

ARTICHOKE.

Large Green Globe. Pkt., 10c.; oz., 25c.; lb., $2.50.

ARTICHOKE ROOTS.

Three bushels will seed an acre.

Jerusalem. This variety is not produced from seed. They are sometimes used as a table vegetable when pickled, but their greatest value is for feeding stock. They are the best hog-food known and are now attracting much attention on account of their great fattening properties, great productiveness (over one thousand bushels having been grown on an acre), and ease with which they can be grown. They need not be dug in the fall; the hogs should be turned in on them, and will help themselves by rooting for them. One acre will keep from twenty to thirty head in fine condition from October until April, except when the ground is frozen too hard for them to root. They are also said to be a preventive of cholera and other hog diseases. They are also highly recommended for milch cows, increasing the yield of milk and at the same time improving their condition. They are well adapted to any soil where corn or potatoes can be grown. The tubers should be cut same as potatoes, one eye to a cut being sufficient, planted in April or May, in rows three feet apart and two feet in the rows, and covered about two inches deep. To destroy them, they should be plowed under when the plant is about a foot high, at which time the old tuber has decayed and new ones are not yet formed. They can be shipped at any time during the season, as they are not injured by freezing. Lb., 35c.; 4 lbs., $1.00, post-paid; by freight or express, peck, $1.00; bush., $3.00; bbl. of 3 bush, $7.50.

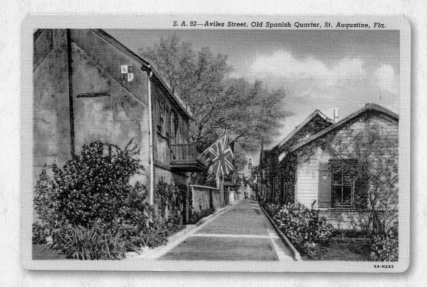

S. A. 92—Aviles Street, Old Spanish Quarter, St. Augustine, Fla.

6A-H283

COURT, PONCE DE LEON HOTEL, ST. AUGUSTINE, FLA.

115677

D. C. 107—Widener Fountain
and Club House Lawn
Hialeah Race Course

In the sixteenth century the Spanish settled Florida, first at St. Augustine. The subtropical climate allowed for the introduction of citrus and other familiar European edibles, which were joined with native flora. The influence of Spanish culture continues in both gardens and architecture. Early twentieth-century postcards picture Old St. Augustine, the Ponce de Leon Hotel, now re-purposed as part of Flagler College, and the still vibrant Hialeah Race Course. *The Cottage Collection,*

SPANISH INFLUENCES

Fifteenth and sixteenth century Spaniards introduced many familiar crops to Florida Indians so that by the time the Dutch, Swedes, and English arrived they discovered that the Indians were growing cucumbers and watermelons, the latter of African origin. In retrospect, it is curious to note that North American Indians did not grow the potato —a native of South America, nor its relative the tomato. Indians sensibly grew their gardens in rows, sometimes fenced. Few northern Indians grew flowers, as such, but many encouraged those wildflowers that they found especially attractive, such as the Black-eyed Susan (*Rudbeckia hirta*) and the New England Aster (*Symphyotrichum novae-angliae*). Native American gardens and what we would call grain fields were united in one. Within the European context the term garden is separated from large-scale plantations, *i.e.* wheat fields, corn fields, bean fields, flax fields. Gardens are contained, often enclosed or fenced, with beds containing vegetables and flowers along with, perhaps, fruitful shrubs and a few fruit trees.

The Spanish, especially Jesuit missionaries, introduced a variety of fruits and vegetables into Florida and presumably introduced their garden forms as well. However, the walled or courtyard garden of arid Spain would not prove viable in the humid American south. On the Pacific coast, where the Mediterranean climate favored the sheltering walls of the enclosed garden, the story was different. It is in California, and especially in the surviving missions, that we see remnants of the form of the Spanish garden in America, often as a restoration, as well as in sites in Texas, Arizona, and New Mexico.

SPANISH PATIO, MISSION INN, RIVERSIDE, CALIFORNIA—7

The Mission Inn and nearby streets in Riverside, California, reflect the traditions of Spanish architecture and horticulture, which place a premium on the protection of walled patios and areas of shade from the hot sun. *The Cottage Collection.*

5312. IN THE GARDEN.

SB-51 THE SANTA BARBARA MISSION AND GROUNDS, FOUNDED 1786

A-13933

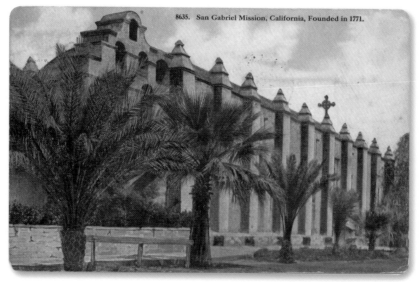

8635. San Gabriel Mission, California, Founded in 1771.

The climate of California very closely resembles that of Spain, and the Franciscan Fathers, who established the mission system in the eighteenth and early nineteenth centuries, introduced many Old World plants and cloistered gardens into "New Spain." Date trees line a façade of San Gabriel Mission. *The Cottage Collection.*

On Southern plantations African slaves were often allotted plots for growing some of their own food. Here they cultivated some crops they knew from their homelands, including peanuts, okra, and watermelons, all of which were to become part of our mainstream diets. Also carrying over from Africa is the bare earth, swept yard around traditional homes, which was originally meant to keep snakes at bay in Africa and served a similar purpose in parts of the American South. With freedom, unique ornamental gardens, documented in Vaughn Sills's *Places for the Spirit: Traditional African American Gardens*, emerged primarily in the Deep South. "These landscapes have a unique historical significance," writes Sills, "due to the design elements and spiritual meanings that have been traced to yards and gardens of American slaves and further back to their prior African heritage." The gardens exist "... in the spirit of 'outsider art' ... these gardens have a unique aesthetic and cultural significance." They also, alas, are a "... disappearing element of African American culture."

Calla lilies (*Zantedeschia aethiopica*) were introduced from Africa to Spain and then to California, where they thrive. Early twentieth-century California cottages combined Spanish and arts and crafts architecture and took advantage of miraculous growing conditions.
The Cottage Collection.

Artist Gerald Cassidy (1879–1934) painted his patio garden in Santa Fe, New Mexico. *Private collection.*

Left, top to bottom

A glamorous Spanish-inspired garden in Santa Barbara, California, was painted by Colin Campbell Cooper (1856-1937). *Private collection.*

The enclosed garden of the 1827 Casa de Estudillo in San Diego, California, contains a traditional *horno* or out-of-doors bake oven. *Irwin Richman*

A 1920s Spanish-style house in Los Angeles includes a planted, walled entry court. Note the lush banana tree to the left. *Irwin Richman.*

The patio of the Palace of the Governors in Santa Fe, New Mexico. Portions of the building date to the seventeenth century. *Irwin Richman.*

In desert areas of the Southwest, cactus and other succulents are often incorporated into garden designs. American plants were also sent back to Spain, where many flourish in gardens—and others have become weeds. *The Cottage Collection.*

In autumn the sight of drying chili peppers is familiar in the American Southwest. The plants from the genus *Capsicum* are American natives, which have been spread worldwide. *The Cottage Collection.*

A private garden in Las Cruces, New Mexico, combines Southwestern regional gardening practices, some Spanish and Indian, with pure fantasy. *Irwin Richman.*

ANGLO-DUTCH TRADITIONS

Because the preponderance of seventeenth, eighteenth, and early nineteenth century settlers of North America were of British Islands origin, gardens reflective of their culture were dominant. Here we are introduced to the Anglo-Dutch garden tradition, which is reflective of the long-standing close trade and cultural ties between the two European cultural areas. For example, the mother of Pennsylvania founder William Penn was Margaret Jasper, a daughter of a wealthy Rotterdam merchant. Her husband, Admiral Sir William Penn, was a confidant of English royalty. When members of the interrelated Dutch Royal Family, the House of Orange, William III and Mary ascended the British throne in 1689, they brought with them a large retinue including gardeners, and the Dutch influence on English gardens was solidified. Anglo-Dutch gardens tended to be symmetrical; in the simplest form they were often cruciform, although other garden layouts might include a variety of other shapes. Beds were often bordered in boxwood (most commonly, *Buxus sempervirens*) or other easily contained shrubs. Paths between beds allowed for easy access by gardeners and were most commonly bare earth or gravel. In areas where shellfish were common, crushed shells were used on paths. In more deluxe instances, paths might be paved with brick or even stone. The path and structure made especial sense when hand labor was the principal tool, but declined with large-scale market gardening, where animals were used. The later rototiller and confined geometric beds do not comfortably coexist.

The vision of old English gardens is tied to images of countryside and thatched cottages as depicted in early twentieth-century postcards. *The Cottage Collection.*

Seventeenth-century gardening in England employed geometrically defined beds as seen in an illustration from Thomas Hill, *The Gardener's Labyrinth of 1652. Private collection.*

Formal seventeenth-century English gardens are strongly influenced by Dutch garden practices and are often referred to as "Anglo Dutch gardens." *Private collection.*

The Apothecaries' Garden (now the Chelsea Physic Garden) in London, seen in 1751, strongly reflects the precedents of the Leiden garden shown on page 41. *Private collection.*

The re-created gardens at Plimouth Plantation represent adaptations of the English traditional forms. *Plimouth Plantation, Inc.*

The gardens of Pennsbury Manor, the re-created estate of William Penn (1644–1718) in Bucks County, Pennsylvania, represents the Anglo Dutch influences of the advanced garden tastes of England's upper class. A well is at the center of the kitchen gardens. *Pennsbury Manor of the Pennsylvania Historical and Museum Commission.*

The English and other Europeans introduced the honeybee and apiary culture into the New World. A favored nectar source for bees, the red clover (*Trifolium pratense*), is also a European import. The modern bee boxes or hives are on the grounds of the Landis Valley Village and Farm Museum. *Honey graphic, the Cottage Collection.*

Among the finest re-creations of Anglo Dutch gardens in America, and the most influential, are those at Colonial Williamsburg. The in-town George Wythe garden is one of the most beautiful. The most authentic was the now-discontinued garden at Carter's Grove Plantation, which was primarily devoted to foodstuffs. The roses, shown with a wattle or woven fence in the background, were grown primarily for making rose water and for other use in cooking and baking. *Irwin Richman*.

The Frogmore Kitchen Gardens at Windsor were established by Queen Victoria to supply the Royals with fruits and vegetables. They continued the Anglo Dutch garden traditions into the nineteenth century. *Private collection.*

Mr. Cason's Vegetable Garden at Georgia's Callaway Gardens is the American garden in current operation closest to the scale and excellence of maintenance that Frogmore illustrated. It was the last major garden feature created by the garden's founder Cason J. Callaway (1894–1961). *Irwin Richman.*

As America approached the Centennial of the Declaration of Independence in 1876 there was a revival among hobbyists of an interest in "old-fashioned" gardens. What is now called the colonial revival began in earnest and manifested itself in America's architecture and gardens. The nostalgia for and glorification of our Colonial past reached its apogee with happenings in the capital of the former Colony of Virginia, Willliamsburg, named in honor of the Anglo-Dutch King William III. Beginning in the late 1920s, thanks to the support of John D. Rockefeller Jr. and his family, the entire historic area of Williamsburg was being restored to its perceived historic appearances. Because Mrs. Rockefeller (Abby Aldrich) was especially interested in gardens, great attention was paid to them, although an inordinate amount of space, as later research has shown, was given to ornamentals rather than food. Widely publicized, Williamsburg became a style and a brand for what the perfect Colonial-style home and garden should look like. The influence continues today.

The Dutch style garden, a re-creation at Philipsburg Manor in Sleepy Hollow, New York, grows in front of the manor house built in the seventeenth century. *Historic Hudson Valley.*

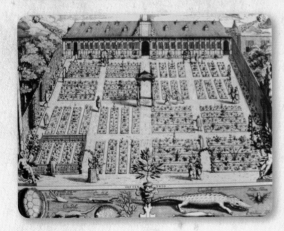

Left, top to bottom | Dutch gardens borrowed from the formality and style of Italian and French gardens. The garden at Huis ten Bosch, painted in the seventeenth century, shows Italianate influences. The seventeenth-century *Hortus Botanicus* (botanical garden) at Leiden in the Netherlands grew plants in a geometrically organized fashion. Gardeners tend a sixteenth-century walled garden in the low countries. *Private collections.*

Right, top to bottom | The Long Walk in the gardens of the Van Cortlandt Manor in New York's Hudson River Valley was created in the eighteenth century, following Dutch and English precedents. *Irwin Richman.*

A fourteenth-century French medicinal garden is walled and geometric. *Private collection.*

Above and right | The French garden style reached its peak in the seventeenth century with the vast grounds of the Palace of Versailles. Everywhere are grand vistas, formal parterres, and water features. *Private collections.*

The vast Orangerie at Versailles, built by Jules Hardouin Mansart between 1684 and 1686, winters 1,000 tender trees planted in boxes. It would be the model for many others built on private estates in Europe and the United States. *Irwin Richman.*

FRENCH VEGETABLE GARDENS

The French vegetable garden or, *jardin potager*, is a symmetric garden often combining flowers along with the esculents, frequently with vegetable plants arranged so that they create elegant patterns. Very few, if any, potagers remain with a history in America, but many modern ones are laid out and are widely praised in popular magazines. Perhaps the finest historically sourced American potager, on the grounds of the Hagley Museum and Library in Wilmington, Delaware, is a re-creation of what can be deemed as Éleuthère Irénée du Pont de Nemours's (1771–1834) elaborate potager. After his death and until 1890 it was refined by his daughter, Victorine.

The *Hameau de la Reine* at Versailles is a rustic retreat created for Queen Marie Antoinette where she and her friends could play at the rustic life. It featured meadows, a farmhouse, and a vegetable garden. *Irwin Richman*.

A private American garden influenced by the French *potager*. *Private collection*.

The French vegetable garden or *jardin potager* often mixes flowers, vegetables, and fruits grown decoratively. The re-created garden of Éleuthère Irénée du Pont de Nemours (1771–1834) near Wilmington, Delaware, is the finest of its type in America. It features shaped or topiaried fruit trees as well as fruit trees espaliered on a trellis tunnel. *Irwin Richman*.

THE PENNSYLVANIA GERMAN GARDEN

Heritage garden forms lasted longest among the Pennsylvania Germans or the Pennsylvania Dutch, who have been characterized as a "persistent minority." Indeed they never completely died out. There are two major divisions among the Pennsylvania Germans. The first are the church people—Lutheran, Reformed, Moravians, and a smatterings of Catholics, who emigrated mostly for economic reasons from a Europe suffering from many dislocations. It is important to remember that prior to 1870 there was no country called Germany, and European borders in general were often redrawn accordingly. Alsace, in modern France, was a German state, as were parts of modern Poland. The church people came mostly from the region near Heidelberg called the Palatinate or *die Pfalz*, from Alsace, and a few came from Austria as well. The second group are the sectarians—the Amish, Mennonites, and Schwenkfelders, along with a few Jews, who came mostly to escape religious persecution. Many Amish and Mennonites came from the German-speaking cantons or states of Switzerland. Less than ten percent of the traditional Pennsylvania German population is sectarian. Co-author Mike Emery's family is a mixture of Amish, church people, and Quaker.

"Pennsylvania German" or "Pennsylvania Dutch" is a question of semantics. Co-author Irwin Richman married into a purebred Pennsylvania German family whose ancestors arrived in America in the 1760s from die Pfalz. His father-in-law, the Reverend Eugene Oscar Steigerwalt (1905–1994) would proudly proclaim himself a "Dutchman" and, indeed, most Pennsylvania Germans comfortably use the "Dutch" identifier. Others felt differently. Bucks County artist and art school founder Walter Emerson Baum (1884–1956), like Pastor Steigerwalt, was born of Palatine ancestry but he hated "Dutch" and insisted on "German," only accepting "Dutch" during World War II. Europe had its *Deutschlanden*, the lowlands near the sea, including the modern Dutch of Holland, *Deutsch* is easily corrupted into "Dutch." The term "Pennsylvania German" is a late-nineteenth century phrase that a scholarly world introduced to delineate these unique Americans. The commonplace definition of who is considered Pennsylvania German, or "Dutch," is that they are descendants of the complex, mostly German-speaking peoples who arrived in America before 1800. No one commonly uses the very accurate and descriptive term "*Pennsylvanisch Deitsch.*"

Pennsylvania German gardens have a very distinctive form and in settlements the gardens often came before the permanent homes. When emigrants opened their precious travel chests, cuttings and seeds often came out first, truly transplants from the homeland. The oldest surviving plans that relate to the evolution of the Pennsylvania German kitchen garden are the medicinal gardens of the Benedictine cloisters of Saint Gall in Switzerland and Reichenau in Germany. Plans dating from the 1600s for their *berbularis*, or herb gardens, called for laying out a quadrant *innenbof* [courtyard] or *atrioluse* [small atrium] to be divided into garden beds. In turn, this plan was copied and adopted in cloisters and monasteries throughout Europe. By the Middle Ages, the enclosed kitchen garden laid out in quadrants with raised beds and pathways between them was widely promoted as the most efficient way of providing the vegetable needs for a household. By the Renaissance, city views show that this type of garden was widely used in urban settings as well. It was this tried-and-true garden form that immigrants from what now constitutes modern Germany and Switzerland brought with them to Pennsylvania.

Cabbage is an important crop among the Germans on both sides of the pond. *Master of All He Surveys* was painted in Germany by Joseph Molitar Von Mahfeld (1856–1890). *The Cabbage Patch* was painted in Europe by American artist Henry Mosler (1844-1920). *Private collections.*

Beans, peas, onions, and asparagus grow in a contemporary garden in the Pfalz, the German region homeland to many Pennsylvania Germans. *Lee Stoltzfus.*

The traditional Pennsylvania German garden form evolved from the courtyard gardens of monasteries. The design for a wealthy person's enclosed garden from seventeenth-century Ulm is reproduced from Johann Furthenbach's *Architectura Privata*, circa 1641. *The Cottage Collection*.

Some early German gardens had irrigation channels. On this side of the Atlantic we have no record of their use in gardens but irrigated meadows were common. The figure on the right in this 1598 illustration is grafting a tree. *The Cottage Collection*.

To this day, many Pennsylvania Germans retain a closeness to the soil that goes beyond mere occupation. It has religious overtones. It might relate to their social history or their sense of place. Scholar John Frantz, a longtime faculty member now retired from the Pennsylvania State University and an authority on Pennsylvania German history, is an avid gardener who professes that "he can't help himself" when spring comes. His garden has strong traditional overtones.

Co-author Richman's father-in-law, a Lutheran minister, prided himself on his gardening abilities, often recounting his past gardening feats. His children, who had often been pressed to help weed or harvest, are less lyrical in their remembrances. His daughter Leah, a very casual gardener at best, several years ago reported that her son, John, "... seems to have inherited Daddy's love of a vegetable garden, … go figure!" Genes will out.

In addition to a passion for gardening, the Pennsylvania Germans maintain a strong desire to preserve ancestral seeds, perhaps summed up in the saying, *Gude Sume, Gude Gaarde* (good seeds, good garden). An extraordinary number of American heirloom seed varieties bear the prefix "German" or "Amish." This phenomenon will be discussed in detail in a later chapter.

Interest in the plants that the Pennsylvania Germans traditionally grew in their gardens became of concern to the scholarly community as the old ways were disappearing. Probably the most inclusive list of plants grown in Dutch gardens was published in 1923 by David E. Luck and the Reverend Thomas R. Brendle. The pioneer modern scholar of the German garden is Alan G. Keyser, whose seminal article, "Gardens and Gardening Among the Pennsylvania Germans," appeared in 1971. Important research and publication goes on, especially in the various books by William Woys Weaver.

In sharp distinction to the general American concept of vegetable gardening as a male pursuit, the Pennsylvania German kitchen garden was always considered to be primarily the woman's province, as an extension of the house. The men in the family were expected to build the garden, spread manure on the beds in fall, and turn over the soil for spring planting, but the women and children planted, weeded, watered, and harvested. The most common Pennsylvania Dutch garden contained four symmetrical raised garden beds, although six, eight, or other even numbers of beds were not unknown.

An article that reviewed the life of Joseph F. Beiler, an Amish farmer and founder of the Amish newspaper *The Diary* who died in 2004 and also celebrated his wife of sixty years, Sadie Smucker Beiler, whose life revolved around the garden and the farm, Samuel Stoltzfus wrote:

...seeing Joe as a young farmer in his fields …. Sadie, then an energetic young housewife was gardening, housekeeping, and helping in the barn as much as possible. … Sadie loved farm work, cows, and horses. Now as a farmer's wife she had the life of her dreams.

Gardens were built in multiples of eleven feet, with the most common dimensions being fifty-five or sixty-six feet square. The beds themselves were divided by narrow paths, no wider than eighteen inches, usually simply packed earth. Often the gardener's regular attention to the beds was all that was required to keep the weeds in the path to a minimum. If a tool were used it was a *breed hock* or broad hoe, which could scrape the paths clean. In areas where sawdust or tan bark was easily available it might be laid on the path. In very rare instances paving might be used. With the common use of the lawn mower, some grass paths were also known—but this would be late in the story. Maintaining grass paths is very labor-intensive and grass spreading into the beds is always a problem.

People, some in costume, work in traditional
raised-bed German gardens from Frankfurt,
Germany, in 1546 to the contemporary United
States *1546 print, The Cottage Collection.*

The surface of the individual beds was raised, usually, six to eight inches. Very commonly the sides sloped at about a sixty degree angle, which was kept as uniform as possible. Gardeners with these raised earth beds spent a lot of time keeping their edges straight. Equally ancient was the custom of bordering the beds with planks, usually of first growth pine, chestnut, or oak, eight to twelve inches high. These good woods would last for twenty to thirty years, which is much longer than modern lumber. The boards would be held in place by stakes of the same woods, placed every few feet. In rare cases the beds might be bordered in English or American boxwood. At least one such garden survived into the twentieth century. In Anglo-American culture, as noted above, boxwood-lined beds became a hallmark of the colonial revival garden. This became even more prevalent with the resurrection of Colonial Williamsburg in Virginia.

In many cases the four bed garden was standard for the nuclear family. When a farmer died and his widow remained on the farm (in the *grossmutter*'s house or in a portion of the family home bequeathed to her), she would often also be willed part of the garden, at which time the number of beds would often be increased. For example, Jacob Landis's will, probated in Lancaster County, Pennsylvania, in 1848, was typical in making sure his widow would be well taken care of after his death, as long as she remained a widow. If she should remarry, she would lose all of her endowed rights:

I give and bequeath unto my beloved wife Elizabeth all my household furniture, kitchen utensils and such other articles, things and effects used in the family, as she may choose to have, as much of the provision on hand, as she may necessarily want; and one cow and one hog, her choice of the stock on hand and the sum of twenty dollars lawful money of the United States to be paid to her by my herein after named executors, as soon as conveniently can be after my decease; all which I give and bequeath unto my dear wife Elizabeth, to her and to her heirs and assigns forever.

I do further give and bequeath unto my said beloved wife Elizabeth, as long as she is my widow, the use and occupation of the one story new brick dwelling house wherein I now reside and right, liberty and privilege to use the wash house near said dwelling house, the waters of the pump and the bakeoven at or near the same from time to time, during the aforesaid period, as she may have occasion for the same; and shall have the use of so much of the garden adjoining the said dwelling house as she may choose to have, not exceeding one half thereof, and shall have the use of the hogsty near said house for and during the time aforesaid. And I do further give and bequeath unto my said beloved wife Elizabeth the following articles and things to be delivered to her yearly and every year as long as she is my widow, by my herein after named son Jacob Landis, his heirs or assigns, in proper time and season in each year out of the lands and premises herein after devised to him and them that is to say; ten bushels of good clean oats, four bushels of good potatoes, and one hind quarter of good fat beef, weighing not less than one hundred pounds including the kidney tallow; as much apple butter and as many summer and winter apples, and other fruit growing on the herein after devised premises as she may need; and as much fuel, coal and wood, as she may want from time to time for her use, the wood to be cut short and split find fit for her use and laid or placed together with the coal near the door of her said dwelling house convenient for her to get it. And my said son Jacob Landis his heirs or assigns shall feed and pasture, stable and litter my said wife's one cow for her use and benefit during the time aforesaid on the premises hereinafter devised to him and

A modern schematic illustration of the basic four square Pennsylvania German garden clearly illustrates the form's composition. Note that the central bed, which typically grew ornamentals, was not usually raised. *Lancaster-York Heritage Region.*

them, like his or their own; and shall supply her hogsty with litter and clean the same, and manure her part of the garden, from time to time during the above mentioned period as often as necessary; and shall furnish her with a safe and good horse creature. …

Earliest gardens were probably protected by a woven or wattle fence, but these were soon replaced with a pale or picket fence, which was inexpensive in an age of abundant first-growth lumber, long lasting, and, most important of all, allowed for a free flow of air in the garden, very necessary in the humid summers of Eastern and South Central Pennsylvania. When building a fence, posts were placed in the ground at eleven-foot intervals and an eleven-foot panel of the fence, in Dutch *ein gfach*, was attached to them. The principal function of the fence was to keep animals out, particularly rabbits, but also skunks, raccoons, groundhogs, and especially chickens—all notorious crop destroyers. Deer, the bane of modern gardeners, were no problem for the Pennsylvania Germans, who simply slaughtered them for meat whenever they could. Irwin Richman's 103-year-old mother-in-law, Florence Caroline Steigerwalt, who grew up on a traditional Dutch farm straddling Carbon and Schuylkill counties, which included a fruit orchard, recalls that she never saw a wild deer until she was in her twenties. Garden fences, therefore, did not have to be excessively high. The fence, in most cases, was between thirty-six and forty inches high, and the rough cut pales typically extended into the ground or into a sill board that extended into the ground. Additionally, the pales were close together, seldom more than two inches apart, and the top of each one was cut into a point, symmetrically or on a diagonal, which allowed rainwater to drain easily, preventing the wood from rotting, and also made the fence uncomfortable for an animal to rest its neck or a small human to scale and unpleasant for a marauding cow to graze over. Pales were attached by two nails, one near the top, one near the bottom, to the supporting rails, and the nails were reused when the fence needed to be replaced. There was generally only one opening into a garden that was hung with a gate, *s daerche* or *s daerli* in dialect. The aperture would be made slightly larger than the wheelbarrow used for the garden.

By the nineteenth century it was common to whitewash the picket fence annually, and on a well-kept farm whitewash would also be applied to the bases of grape vines and the trunks of fruit trees, as well as many outbuildings including milk houses and pig pens.

The prime function of the raised beds was to promote easy drainage, but they also allowed for conditioning the soil so that the gardener could grow a larger assortment of crops than would be successful otherwise. Because of the quick drainage of the beds, cool soil vegetables like English (sweet) peas, lettuces, spring onions, and radishes could be planted earlier than they could in the surrounding fields, where wet conditions would rot the precious seed. If the soil on the farm or homestead was heavy clay, or rocky, one or more beds might be filled with sieved soil, enhanced with sand, so that root crops like carrots could grow to their full potential. Great attention was paid to keeping the soil in beds friable and loose. Cultivation was never done with a plow or a cultivator, but always with a hoe, typically a *zink hock*, a hoe that has two heavy tines spaced three inches apart, which are directly opposite a three-inch wide blade. Missed weeds would be hand-pulled. Gardens were never worked when the soil was wet. When planting rows, boards were often placed across the edging planks so that the gardener could lean into the bed without having to rest the weight of her hand on the soil. Many gardeners preferred not to work in the heat of midday or when plants were wet.

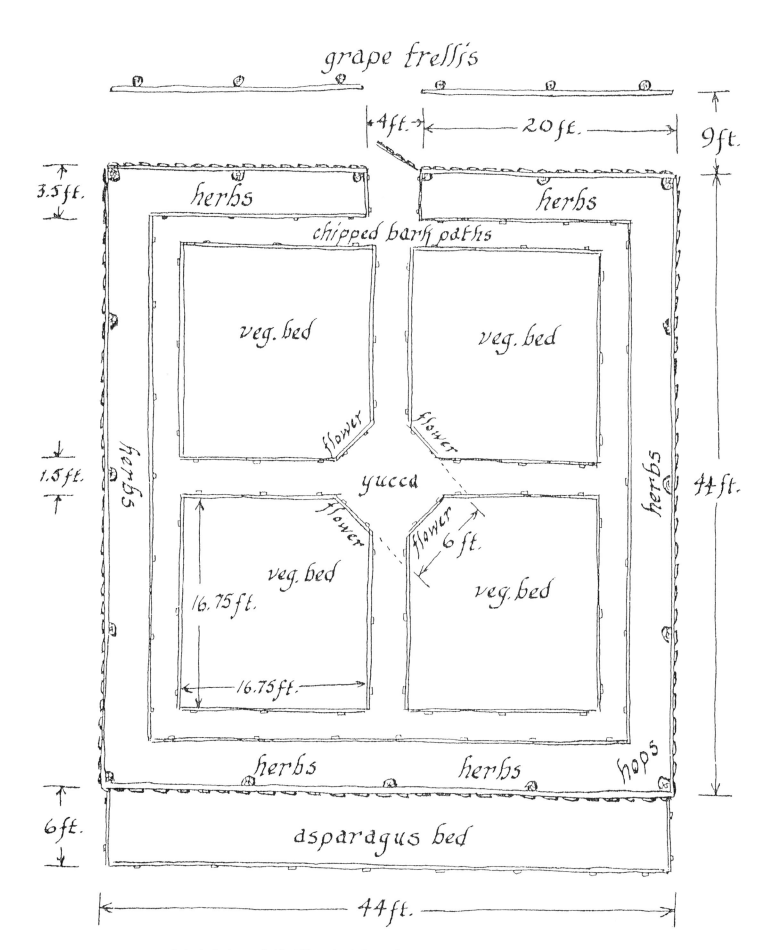

grape trellis

4 ft.

20 ft.

9 ft.

3.5 ft.

herbs

herbs

chipped bark paths

veg. bed

veg. bed

herbs

herbs

flower

flower

1.5 ft.

yucca

flower

flower

6 ft.

veg. bed

veg. bed

44 ft.

16.75 ft.

16.75 ft.

hops

herbs

herbs

6 ft.

asparagus bed

44 ft.

A plan for the layout of a 44' x 44' Pennsylvania German four square garden serves as a template to create
your own. Paths were traditionally hard packed bare earth; now most people prefer to use a mulch.

What was grown in the kitchen garden varied with time, but it is important to note that a differentiation was made among garden crops. Staples, such as cabbages, potatoes, turnips, and field peas, were usually grown in a larger secondary vegetable patch known as *die Lott* or *s schtick*, where the men were more actively involved. Indeed, the kitchen garden was always close by so the housewife could easily keep watch over it from the house. It was most commonly either northeast, east, south, or southwest of the house to catch maximum sunlight. Rarely was it located elsewhere. By contrast, die Lott was often placed beyond the barnyard. Being larger, and level or on a slight slope, it was commonly plowed with the use of horses or mules. It is, of course, the inspiration for many male-tended gardens in Dutch country today.

Mennonite Hanna Rittenhouse Clemens (1880–1977) of Montgomery County recalls that in her childhood:

… we had a garden and a patch. And we raised sweet corn and lima bean and all this kept you busy, you know. Now you can go to the store and buy a pack and dump it in the boiler and it's soon fixed. Then you had to plant them and hoe them and pick them and shell them. It's a little bit more work. But they're good.

Generally the kitchen garden provided at least two crops per bed per year. Sometimes, for example, radishes were interplanted with onions before the last hoeing. Besides those already mentioned, favored garden plantings by the early twentieth century included peppers, eggplant, tomatoes, cucumbers, and melons. Spinach and fancy cabbages like crinkled-leaf savoy, were also popular, as were specialty corns, such as popping corn.

Many foursquare gardens were bordered with additional beds that followed the perimeter fencing. The fences could then be used to support vines or brambles. Cucumber vines might be trained on the fence, as were hopvines, the dried flowers of which were used in making bread and beer, as well as for a pillow filling that was highly regarded as a soporific for insomniacs. Often, too, hops might be grown on high poles that would be taken down at harvest time. These border beds might also be used for small fruits like currants or raspberries, or for medicinal or flavoring herbs.

While the layout of the traditional Pennsylvania Dutch garden is derived from the herb gardens of monasteries, the Dutch did not have herb gardens as we understand them. Those are a creation of the colonial revival of the late nineteenth and early twentieth centuries. Traditional German cookery used few flavor enhancers besides salt and pepper (if available). The most commonly grown seasonings were onions, parsley, sage, and dill, which was highly favored for pickling. Saffron, the product of *Crocus savitus*, an autumn-blooming flower that is notoriously laborious to harvest, was also very commonly cultivated, although today it is grown by few gardeners, most of whom are Mennonites and by one of the last of the commercial growers, Robert Martin Keen, using land near Landisville that has been in his family since 1725. The other highly favored condiment plant, horseradish, was rarely grown in a garden because of its invasive nature. The same is true of many members of the mint family, which the Germans brewed into teas and gave great medicinal credits to as well. There were exceptions, of course. Mrs. Clemens recalls that her mother's garden:

… had that wooly balsam tea, the wooly mint, and we had the red stem mint. And we had sage and we had rue in the garden. That rue was so bitter. It's very bitter. Oh, thyme. We had thyme. We made some thyme tea too. That's good with doughnuts. We drank thyme tea with doughnuts.

A raised bed garden was photographed by Henry K. Landis (1865–1955) in Church Town in Lancaster County, Pennsylvania, in the 1930s. The garden is fitted with boards to protect the soil from compaction when the gardeners needed access. A row of gladiolus (*Gladiolus x hortulanus*) is in the left center. The Dutch enjoyed the lush flower spikes that lent themselves to being grown in rows like vegetables. Many were also raised for market in truck patches.

Women traditionally cared for the Pennsylvania German kitchen gardens as shown in a detail of a large farm drawing by Ferdinand A. Brader (1833–after 1896) in the collection of the Landis Valley Village and Farm Museum.

Two women and a boy pose in a large truck patch or *die Lott* in central Pennsylvania, circa 1900. *The Cottage Collection*.

The rare Pennsylvania Dutch Roman Catholic sometimes placed a potted rosemary in the center of a foursquare garden, but its significance was religious, associated with the Virgin Mary, not necessarily culinary. Along these lines, Pennsylvania Dutch Protestants often planted an Adam and Eve plant (*Yucca filamentosa*) in the middle of their gardens. However, how this American native plant came to be considered an expression of Protestant faith is not known.

Traditionally, as noted earlier, the Pennsylvania Dutch garden was placed on level or gently sloping ground, although the archaeologically correct, re-created garden at Burnside Plantation, a Moravian site in Bethlehem, Pennsylvania, is on a steep terraced site. Most important was the availability of water, for raised gardens drained so well that they needed to be watered more frequently than did flat gardens. Pennsylvania German farms were invariably laid out on east-west axis, with the house and barn facing south (as noted earlier) and the garden was usually placed near the kitchen door, where it could share a water source, generally a well or spring, with the house. A garden needs at least one inch of water per week, so the chore could be arduous indeed in times of drought, when it might be necessary to fill and haul buckets from more distant water sources. Watering cans were in use early but considered a luxury until inexpensive machine-made galvanized-metal ones became widely available about 1900. Watering a garden was usually a chore assigned to children.

Ellen Gehret uncovered a rather unusual method of watering plants growing on hills, according to Alan G. Keyser in "Gardens and Gardening Among the Pennsylvania Germans" in *Pennsylvania Folklife*. An earthen crock was placed next to each hill and a woolen rag was put into the crock with one end in the water and the other end laid on the hill where the plants were growing. The water then wicked from the crock to the plants. A woolen rag had to be used because no other fabric would wick as well. This was not a common practice, but it was used in the upper end of Montgomery County, and Ellen Gehret found two informants who had seen this used when they were younger. North of Boyertown in Berks County there was, until several years ago, a garden with pale fence around it, and on the fence were hung upside down on the pales many glass jars and earthen crocks. These we always felt were just the applebutter crocks in storage, but they may have been the irrigation crocks and jars for watering by the wick method.

Views of the Kelly farm in Union County and the Hummel Farm in Snyder County, both in Pennsylvania, are late nineteenth-century pen and ink drawings showing fenced traditional gardens. They were drawn by an essentially unknown artist, Herman Markert. *Jim Bohn.*

Common garden tools include a straight line (a string holder), dibbles for planting seeds and transplanting small plants, cultivators, spades, a spading fork, and hoes. All are in the Landis Valley Village and Farm Museum Collection.

The Pennsylvania Dutch were among the first farmers to barn, pen, and pasture their animals, practices that allowed them to collect manure, which they applied liberally to both gardens and fields. They did not use compost, but they often placed their garden near the pigpen, chicken yard, or rabbit hutches so that these animals could convert less palatable garden produce into manure. Among the most dedicated of gardeners, different manures were, and are, preferred for particular crops. Pig manure was especially favored, but some believed that it made the soil too hard. The problem could be dealt with by adding wood ash from the stove to the soil as well. The best day for this was, of course, Ash Wednesday.

Flowers, per se, had little place in Pennsylvania Dutch kitchen gardens originally, although some plants we consider ornamental were grown for their food value. Nasturtiums, for instance, were often raised for their buds, which were pickled to provide a caper substitute; the tender leaves of calendulas, or pot marigolds (*Calendula officinalis*) were eaten as a vegetable and the flowers were used as a dyestuff. Occasionally, French marigolds (*Tagetas patula*), which the Germans called, in translation, "stinky flowers," were grown among beans to repel beetles. In this vein, it is important to remember that although the Pennsylvania Dutch, until the twentieth century, had to contend with fewer garden pests than we do today, the problem has always existed. On occasion they used lethal, but organic, substances such as tobacco dust and highly toxic arsenic-based compounds to deter insects, but a good deal of pest control was purely mechanical; the women and children hand-picked insects, snails, and slugs, which is still the most effective organic method of pest control.

The traditional Pennsylvania Dutch garden was eventually abandoned because of increasing interaction with the "English" world and the rising importance of commercial seed houses and commercial or truck farming. The final blow was the widespread availability of the rototiller after World War II. When power machinery entered the picture, vegetable gardening among nonsectarian Pennsylvania Dutch appears to have shifted to men.

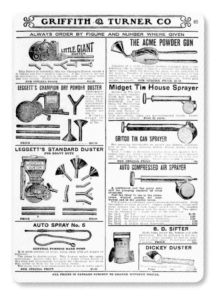

Chemical warfare was used by traditional farmers from the eighteenth century forward. The tools of the attack became ever more varied and efficient by the twentieth century.

The Pennsylvania Dutch kitchen garden form was in flux as it declined. A first step was to remove the side paths and to make the garden into a bilaterally symmetric expression. Additionally, gardens would admit more flowers and even shrubs, yielding more food production to die Lott. Certainly in town and on prosperous farms more and more vegetables and herbs might be purchased and/or bartered. Farmer Henry H. Landis (1838–1926), the father of the founders of the Landis Valley Village and Farm Museum, kept a diary that is replete with mentions of garden produce, including parsnips that were gifts from neighbors as well as various purchases including strawberries. Flower beds also often existed outside of the kitchen garden itself, especially by the late nineteenth and pre-World War II twentieth centuries. Among Mennonites, especially where the custom of Sunday after-church visits remained strong, flower beds were often planted between the house and the garden, so that even the plainest of the Mennonites could "inadvertently" show off their flowers when showing their relatives and neighbors the kitchen gardens.

When herbs for medicinal or culinary uses were grown in the historic garden they were usually planted in one of the perimeter or outside beds, often one nearest to the gate. Similarly, flowers, if present, would usually be grown in the outside beds as well—often on the opposite side of the gate from the herbs.

The following is a list of plants commonly grown in Pennsylvania Dutch gardens, which is adapted from one compiled by David E. Lick and the Reverend Thomas R. Brendle in 1923 when many gardens and informants not available to later researchers were still about. The list has been also added to by Alan Keyser and others. Of course it is also important to remember that not all of these plants would have been found in any one garden or at any one date.

The Pennsylvania German garden in the press. This artist's rendition of a botanically impossible garden (daffodils and cauliflower blooming at their peak simultaneously!) appeared in the Lancaster, Pennsylvania, *New Era* in 1988. *The Lancaster Newspapers*.

OUTSIDE BED

Agrimony	*Agrimonia*, genus
Asparagus	*Asparagus officinalis*
Asphodel	*Asphodelus luteus*
Avens	*Geum*, genus; *Geum urbanum*
Black Currant	*Ribes nigrum*
Black Raspberry	*Rubus occidentalis*
Blessed Thistle	*Cnicus Benedictus*
Blue Vervain	*Verbena Officinalis*
Boxwood	*Buxus sempervirens*
Calabash	*Lagenaria vulgaris*
Castor Bean	*Ricinus communis*
Catnip	*Nepeta Cataria*
Chamomile	*Anthemis nobilis*
Chives	*Allium Schoenoprasium*
Coltsfoot	*Tussilago Farfara.*
Comfrey	*Symphytum officinale*
Downy Mint	*Mentha alopercuriodes*
Elecampane	*Inuls Helenium*
Feverfew	*Chrysanthemum Parthenium*
Fumitory	*Fumaria officinalis*
Garden Balm	*Melisa officinalis*
Gooseberry	*Ribes reclinatum*
Grape	*Vitis* genus
Ground Almonds	*Cyperus esculentus*
Hellebore	*Helleborus viridis.*
High Blackberries	*Rubus allegheniensis*
Hop	*Humulus Lupulus*
Horehound	*Marrubium vulgare*
Horse Radish	*Radicula Armoracia*
Hyacinth Bean	*Dolichos Lablab*
Hyssop	*Hyssopus officinalis*

Jerusalem Artichoke	*Helianthus tuberosus*
Juneberry	*Amelanchier*, genus
Lady Thistle	*Silybum marianum*
Lavender	*Lavendula vera*
Lilac Bush	*Syringa vulgaris*
Lovage	*Levisticum officinale*
Lungwort	*Pulmonara officinalis*
Masterwort	*Imperatoria Ostruthium*
Meadow Sweet	*Filipendula Ulmarid*
Motherwort	*Leonurus Cardiaca*
Mugwort	*Artemisia vulgaris*
Oswego Tea	*Monarda didyma*
Parsley	*Carum Petroselinum*
Peppermint	*Mentha Piperita.*
Pimpernell	*Pimpinella Saxifraga*
Red Currant	*Ribes vulgare*
Red Raspberry	*Rubus idaeus*
Rhubarb	*Rheum Rhaponticum*
Rue	*Ruta graveolens*
Saffron	*Crocus sativus*
Sage	*Salvia officinalis*
Self-heal	*Prunella vulgaris*
Southernwood	*Artemisia, Abrotanum*
Spearmint	*Mentha spicata*
Speedwell	*Veronica officinalis*
Spurge	*Euphorbia Lathyrus*
Strawberry	*Fragaria*, genus
Sweet Cicely	*Osmorhiza*, genus
Sweet Marjoram	*Origanum Marjorana*
Tansy	*Tanacetum vulgare*
Thyme	*Thymus serpyllum*
Valerian	*Valeriana officinalis*
Wormwood	*Artemisia Absinthium*

FOUR MAIN BEDS

Beans	Bush varieties and occasionally pole beans
Borage	*Borage officinalis*
Cabbage	*Brassica oleracea, Capitata* Group
Caraway	*Carum Carvi*
Carrot	*Daucus Carota*
Catchfly	*Silene inflata*
Cauliflower	*Brassica oleracea, Botrytis* Group
Celery	*Apium graveolens*
Coriander	*Coriander sativium*
Corn Salad	*Valerianella,* genus
Cucumber	*Cucumis sativus*
Endive	*Cichorium Endivia*
English Peas	*Pisum sativum,* and varieties
Fennel	*Foeniculum vulgare*
Ground Cherry	*Physalis,* genus
Job's Tears	*Coix Lachryma-Jobii*
Kohlrabi	*Brassica oleracea, Gongylodes* Group
Lentils	*Lens esculenta*
Lettuce	*Lactuca sativa*
Mammoth Pumpkin	*Cucurbita Maxima* and var.
Multiplier	*Allium Cepa* var. *multiplicans*
Onion	*Allium Cepa*
Orach	*Atriplex hortensis*
Parsnips	*Pastinaca sativa*
Peppers	*Capsicum annum* var.
Popcorn	Var. of *Zea Mays*
Potato	*Solanum tuberosum*
Radish	*Raphanus sativus*
Red Beet	*Beta vulgaris*
Savory	*Satureja Hortensis*
Spinach	*Spinacia oleracea*
Sweet Potato	*Ipomoea batatas*
Tobacco	*Nicotiana,* genus
Tomato	*Lycopersicum esculentum*
Top Onion	*Allium proliferum*
Turnip	*Brassica Rapa*

ORNAMENTALS AND FLOWERS

Amaranth	*Amaranthus* tricolor	Immortelle	*Helichrysum*, genus
Amaranth	*Amaranthus*, genus	Iris	*Iris*, genus
Aster	*Asternovai-angliae*	Japanese Lantern	*Physalis pubescens*
August Lily	*Hosta plantaginea*	Larkspur	*Delphinium*, genus
Bergamot Mint	*Mentha peperita var. citrata*	Leopard Plant	*Farfugium grande*
Birthwort	*Aristolochia Clematitis*	Lily-of-the-Valley	*Convallaria Majalis*
Bleeding Heart	*Dicentra spectabilis*	Madonna Lily	*Lilium candidum*
Calendula	*Calendula officinalis*	Moneywort	*Lysimachia Nummularia*
China Asters	*Callistephus chinensus*	Nasturtium	*Tropaelua Maias*
Chrysanthemum	*Chrysanthemum*, genus	Peony	*Paeonia officinalis* and varieties
Columbine	*Aquilegia*, genus	Periwinkle	*Vinca minor*
Corn Poppy	*Papaver Rhoeas*	Petunia	*Petunia*, genus
Creeping Boys and Girls	*Sedum acre*	Phlox	*Phlox Drummondii*
Daffodil	*Narcissus pseudo narcissus*	Poppy	*Papaver*, genus
Dahlia	*Dahlia variabilis*	Prince's Feather	*Polygonum Orientale*
Day Lily	*Hemerocallis fulva*	Red-Hot-Poker-Plant	*Kniphofia aloides*
Dusty Miller	*Centaurea* and *Cinervaria*	Rose Moss	*Portulaca grandiflora*
French Marigolds	*Tagetas patula*	Rose-of-Heaven	*Agrostemma Coeli-rosa*
Garden Fuchsia	*Fuchsia*, genus	Snapdragun	*Antirrhinum majus*
Garden Orpine	*Sedum purpureum*	Stocks	*Matthiola*, genus
Garden Pinks	*Dianthus Caryphyllus var.*	Summer Cypress	*Kochia scoparia*
Geranium	*Pelargonium*, genus	Sweet Alyssum	*Alyssum maritimum*
Grape Hyacinth	*Muscari botryoides*	Sweet William	*Dianthus barbatus*
Hollyhock	*Althea rosea*	Tiger Lily	*Lilium tigrinum*
Honesty	*Lunaria biennis*	Violet	*Viola*, blue species
Houseleek	*Sempervivum tectorum*	Wall Flower	*Cheiranthus cheiri*
Hyacinth	*Hyacinthus orientalis*	Woodland Tulip	*Tulipa sylvestris*

CENTER BED

Adam & Eve Plant	*Yucca filamentosa*
Crown of Thorns	*Berberis*—a cultivated dwarf form
Hollyhock	*Atheo rosea*
Pansy	*Viola* tricolor
Rosemary	*Rosemarius officinalis*
Saffron	*Crocus sativus*

The Pennsylvania Germans have been traditionally both religious and superstitious. These were the people, please remember, who gave us the Easter bunny. Accordingly, their beliefs and traditions often governed the dates and ways in which they planted. These mystic rules were followed both by women in their kitchen gardens and men in die Lott. It is fair to assert that traditionally it is probable that every housewife and her husband used some sort of system based on the church calendar and/or the signs of the zodiac in their gardening. Even today many people who prepare their normative looking gardens with a rototiller use such a system. Various old farmers' almanacs continue to be published for and purchased by the traditionally minded.

Before getting to the specifics of the systems, keep in mind that it was absolutely forbidden to work in the garden on the Sabbath, and on Ascension Day. It was often debated as to whether or not it was permissible to work on Good Friday and some of the pious would not work on Saturdays or at least on Saturday afternoons because the sixth day was too close to Sunday. Gardeners also gave themselves every chance to imbue praise of their cleanliness and order with religion. Garden tools were, of course, to be kept clean and shining and shovels were often oiled to prevent them from rusting. Fastnacht grease [used up on Fastnacht day or Shrove Tuesday] was believed not only to preserve the shovel better but to also make it slide easily into the soil and to kill harmful insects in the garden.

Many first-person accounts of growing plants following a mystical system were gathered by folklorist and scholar Alan G. Keyser and appeared in his article "Gardens and Gardening Among the Pennsylvania Germans" in *Pennsylvania Folklife*. His reports are clear, direct, and often intriguing:

From Sam Heller we were able to collect his mother's system. This method of planting by the moon seems to be the most commonly followed. Her two signs for planting in the garden were *zwilling un wog* [Gemini and Libra]. Sam said that his mother told him that "*zwillingdut alles dobble*" [the twins double everything] and in "*wog grickscht alles wider zurick*" [in the scales everything is returned]. From another source we have the type of seeds to be planted on the above days. Things which yield above the ground such as beans and pickles should be planted in the twins because it is the ascent of the moon. Things which grow below the ground such as red beets, radishes, and potatoes should be planted in the scales because it is in the descent of the moon. Sam's mother also liked to transplant her flowers on *der blumme daak* [the flower day, i.e. the sign of the Virgin]. This sign was considered to be good for flowers only, and any vegetables planted in the virgin would only bloom. Nothing was ever to be planted in *der schitz* [Sagittarius—the bowman] because it would "shoot" to seed [there is one exception to this common belief: pole beans should be planted on the bowman so they will go up the pole]. Nothing was planted *uff fisch odder wasserman* [on Pisces or Aquarius] because it would be too wet. Sallie Snyder told me that if you plant red beets in the sign of the fish they will get stringy, and the seeds planted in waterman will rot. Do not plant anything in Scorpio or Capricorn. (Here I have not been able to find reasons or explanations for these beliefs.) *Grebs* (the crab) is also not a good sign for planting, and Emma Becker of Washington Township, Berks County, gave the reason. The "crab walks backwards so the plants will grow backwards or insects will eat the plants." No onions or radishes should be planted in *Leeb* (Leo) because they will have a strong flavor. You may plant in *schofbock* but there is no guarantee of favorable results. Sam Heller did not make any comment on the sign of Taurus nor was I able to find anyone else who could.

Charlie Miller of Bechtelsville uses a different system of planting by the signs of the moon. His appears to take advantage of some of the weak points in the previous system, and also uses its strong points. He, for instance, plants his lettuce and radishes in the "waterman" and "fish" so they will become nice and crisp. Charlie also uses the last day of the "blooming lady" (Virgo) for some of his crops that should bloom in order to bear. This includes sugar peas and cucumbers, but he adds that if you plant on the first *jungfrau* (Virgo) you will get nothing but flowers. He also stated that he likes to plant his potatoes in either the "stonebuck" (Capricornus) or the "scale," and was quick to add that the potatoes planted in "stonebuck gave more than in the scales."

Lizzie Heller of near Walnuttown, Berks County, was able to add this to the list of favorable signs for planting. "*Blans in wider no grichscht wider*" [Plant in Aries and you will receive again]. She also prefers to plant in *schteebock*, [Capricornus] and her beans in the "twins." As everyone else, Mrs. Heller declared that the bowman was a poor sign for planting because "*es schiesst in die heh*" ["it shoots up"].

Keyser points out, too, that many gardeners—yesterday and today—ignored many subtleties and employed "…a very simple system, and use nothing more than the ascent of the moon for planting crops which yield above ground, and crops yielding below the ground in the descent."

Even the most casual of the sign-based gardeners were aware of St. Gertraut's (or St. Gertrude's) Day, which was celebrated on March 17. Traditionally this was the day you planted onions and especially cabbage. "If the cabbage seed were sown on any other day it would have become bug infested." After the great Irish immigration of the 1840s, almanac writers, even German language ones, started using St. Patrick as the marker for March 17. And while the date of March 17 retained its sacred quality for German gardeners, its connection to their past became more obscure.

In the past two decades, there has been a revival of appreciation for the raised-bed garden, both by organic gardeners and by historic sites and museums. A panel of the popular comic strip *Hi and Lois* (Sunday, October 23, 2005) shows Lois working at a raised-bed garden. How more popular culture can you get? Organic gardeners appreciate the virtues of a garden that features the use of manure or compost rather than chemical fertilizer and a form that provides substantial yields in a small area.

Articles on raised-bed, usually boarded, gardens are common in many publications—especially those specializing in organic gardening. Information abounds online. When young tech-savvy Korean-born Jonathan Lee wanted to build a raised bed garden behind his suburban home in Cumberland County, Pennsylvania, he used online sources, including YouTube videos. In traditional fashion, his wife, Maria, is the gardener. She concentrates on hard-to-find Korean vegetables!

For modern home gardeners who want to create a raised-bed garden, there are several caveats. First and most important is that you never use pressure treated lumber for enclosing your beds. Treated lumber often contains arsenic or other toxic substances that can easily contaminate your soil. Modern pine or oak boards tend to rot quickly. Cedar is a long-lasting wood that can be used as can redwood, but use of these woods encourages the cutting of these irreplaceable giant trees. Similar questions can be raised about the use of some tropical woods including fine teak. Very durable, but not as aesthetically pleasing as wood, are plastic boards made for the purpose from recycled milk jugs. They are generally available by mail-order from advertisements in organic gardening magazines and online sources.

For those who are mechanically inclined and do not want to dig their garden each season, the chore can be handled with the new lightweight mini tillers. While museums should be scrupulous about dimensions and path surfaces, home gardeners can be a bit more relaxed. You might want to use an eight-foot multiplier instead of an eleven-foot one.

The beautifully created and maintained garden of leading Pennsylvania German garden designer Lee Stoltzfus
near Lititz, Pennsylvania, is emblazoned with flowers. The gardener in his private paradise in 1997.
Continued on page 68 | *Lee Stoltzfus.*

Sections of prefabricated picket fences come in eight-foot sections. The Lees use PVC hoops and netting to protect their crops. As a caution, if you use prefabricated fencing you will also want to line it with a chicken wire on the inside. Modern picket fences allow too many critters in. Also you might want to make your paths wider for easier maneuvering by you and your garden cart. Additionally, most modern gardeners will want to use mulch on the paths. Today you have the extra advantage of using black plastic or horticultural cloth under your tanbark or other appropriate mulch.

The earliest and best documented German, or Anglo-German, garden is at the remarkable Wyck estate in Germantown. The property, originally covering sixty acres, is today just two and a half acres of gardens and landscaped grounds. Hans Millan (d. 1698), a German Swiss Quaker, bought the first part of the property in 1689 and the farm-into-estate would remain in the family until 1973 when it was opened as a museum. Part of the house Millan and his wife built is incorporated into the great house that was altered into its present form by the great Philadelphia architect William Strickland (1788–1854) in 1824. Very little is known about the grounds in the early period, but it is fair to assume that there were gardens in which to grow vegetables for the family and some herbs for medicine and flavoring. It is also probable that fruit trees were also grown because, quite early, Germantown was known for the quality and variety of its fruits. There were perhaps a few flowers sprinkled here and there, but most of the property was devoted to raising the farm crops of the period.

Documented information about the garden came into focus beginning in the 1790s during the residency of Caspar Wistar Haines (1762–1801) and his wife Hannah Marshall Haines (1765–1828). The full botanic importance of the place comes with the ownership period of their son Reuben (1786–1831) and his bride Jane Bowne (1790–1843), whom he married in 1812. Jane was a Quaker from New York whose family had also been very interested in gardening.

In January 1797, Hannah wrote a very informative letter to young Reuben, then at Westtown School, a Quaker boarding school in Chester County, in which she chats about forcing flowers as well as vegetables:

> Peter desires I will tell thee he has caught two dozen of mice, and he says he takes great care of thy flowers. The daisey's look beautiful and the Hyacinths are blowing—Thy Father had two hot beds made yesterday for Cabbage. He has one box full up, and another saw'd a day or two ago. [original spelling and punctuation]

A month later Hannah could report that the cabbages were flourishing and, surprisingly, that, "… our peas are stuck planted and some of the beans," which suggests that a cold frame was being used. Hannah is also happy to report that one of their "… wall flowers [*Cheiranthus cheiri*] is in bloom." A close relative of the cabbage, the Wallflower was perhaps growing close to a stone wall that enabled it to bloom so early. The Germans, according to printer Christopher Saur, called it *Gelbe Nelken-Viole* and it was prized among colonists both as an ornamental and for various medicinal uses, especially by midwives. In this letter Hannah also lamented that new flower seeds were "too expensive to buy."

In her March letter to Reuben his mother provides especially interesting information when she reports, "Josey has begun to put fresh tan in the garden walks and today planted out some nice sallad plants." The use of tanbark on "garden walks" suggests that there were regular defining paths, which probably means that there was a geometric arrangement of beds of flowers and vegetables in a typical eighteenth-century arrangement. The use of tanbark also reflects the fact that Germantown was a tanning community and, indeed, there were tanneries within smelling distance of Wyck. "Sallad plants" refers to greens either fresh or, more likely, cooked.

Caspar Wistar Haines had inherited Wyck from his mother, Margaret Wistar Haines, who died in Philadelphia during the devastating yellow fever epidemic of 1793. Caspar then moved his own young family out to the Germantown countryside where conditions were healthier, as did George and Martha Washington who rented the Franks (Deshler-Morris) House nearby. Young Haines immediately began to upgrade his family property. He built a brew house in 1794 and a barn in 1796 and he improved existing or, perhaps, created new gardens. As we have seen, he had both hot beds and cold frames, and we know that he exchanged cuttings with his relatives and friends in Germantown. He would also buy about 150 new fruit trees from the pioneering William Prince's nursery in Flushing, New York.

On April 1, 1797, Hannah wrote about the trees and more in one of her regular letters to her son.

…our flowers are all up in the garden, and the tree's are almost ready to Bloom, we have had a fence put up all round, and an arbour for the Honeysuckle to run on, and made it much larger than it was before, so that thee will see many alterraisons when thee visit's us. a fifth day thy Father received from New York one hundred fifty trees—Apples-Peaches-Pears and Plums, so that if we should live a few years we shall have plenty of Fruit—I expect also a large crop of rasberry's but hope by the time our fruit is ripe, we shall have thee to help us eat it…

Hannah's garden description is vivid and clear. It is an admixture of the practical and the ornamental—especially the "arbour for the Honeysuckle" that, following the custom of the time, probably had a seat under it where one could read and enjoy the pleasures of the colorful and productive garden.

When Caspar died in 1801, his son Reuben, then fifteen, was apprenticed to his uncle Christopher Marshall, a Philadelphia merchant. Reuben did not enjoy mercantile pursuits. When he turned "twenty-one, his father's legacy in hand…," historian Sandra Mackenzie Lloyd wrote in *Germantown Green: A Living Legacy of Gardens, Orchards, and Pleasure Grounds* (Wyck Association, Germantown Historical Society, 1982):

Reuben forever left full-time commercial enterprises and dedicated himself instead to "the pursuit of knowledge and the society of genuine friends." Rather than relaxing with the good fortune of his wealth, Reuben devoted his life to self-education particularly in areas of scientific study; to agriculture; to active participation in the Academy of Natural Sciences, the Franklin Institute, the Pennsylvania Horticultural Society, and the Philadelphia Society for Promoting Agriculture; to public service, notably in the implementation of school reforms; to the financial sponsorship of struggling artists and philosophers, including Rembrandt Peale and Bronson Alcott; and to the creation of a healthy, happy and stimulating home for his family.

Reuben's wife Jane was the perfect complement to the country gentleman-scholar who Reuben was becoming. She is described by Lloyd as being, "Well educated and equipped with a quick wit." In addition to being a loving wife and devoted mother she was also creative and her "… passion for gardening complemented her husband's interest in agriculture and natural history."

Two years after their marriage in 1812, the young couple who had first lived in Philadelphia started spending their summers at Wyck, which Reuben had renamed in 1807. The setting was still primarily rural, but the grounds had deteriorated during Hannah's widowhood because they had been rented to tenant farmers for over ten years. In June 1814, Jane wrote to her sister Hannah Collins about summering at Wyck.

…I find our situation here much pleasanter than I anticipated … our outdoor kitchen answers very well. We have not however many beautiful views or a fine garden to show our visitors, as the house is immediately on the street—the gable end of it—and the farm extends behind it—the position of the ground does not admit of much ornament—and that which was once bestowed on it is now almost obliterated by a succession of neglectful tenants—we have plenty of excellent vegetables and there will be plumbs and apples but no peaches—a very pleasant shady yard in front where my little Sarah plays quite half her time and where she is now sitting in a wheelbarrow having just had a ride (here let me acquaint thee that the yard is made private by a stone wall next the street lest thee shd be shocked that we do not more maintain the appearance of citizens) Whilst I am seated in a most delightful hall where we live almost entirely it is 20 feet wide with two huge barn-like doors open to the yard in front and garden back—it is always cool here for there is no glass excepting a single row of panes over each door …

Not until 1824 when the barn-like doors were converted into sliding glass doors by William Strickland would the hall become a conservatory, but serious work on the garden was undertaken almost at once. An attractive garden was wanted. Initially Reuben had a carpenter construct a new arbor in the garden, and they hired a gardener named James to help with the grounds. Within a few years the arbor was covered with a coral honeysuckle on one side and a repeat blooming rose on the other. The weed-choked garden had been reclaimed. As Lloyd noted, in 1818, Jane wrote to Reuben from her family home on Long Island:

… I feel quite a regret that I cannot have a little oversight of the garden—but I do not doubt it will be pleasanter than it ever has been to me—James will not allow us at least to loose one another among the weeds—or suffer them to grow so luxuriantly as to become a hiding place for stolen goods—which thee recollects was the case there years ago—I hope to have honeysuckles and roses planted round the Arbour and Lilacks Snowballs and double Altheas at the end of the new path—if convenient a larch tree somewhere and the Bigonia radicans by those old trees in the front yeard—S. Johnson said last summer she would give me some roots of both common and variegated periwinkle—in the desk I left some poppy seeds that I gathered for sister SHB if these are wanted please take part and send the rest to me …

Clearly the garden was not only being reclaimed, it was being changed from a kitchen garden to a mostly ornamental flower garden. Jane and Reuben, however, had different motivations for the change. Jane was an aesthetician. She loved color and beauty. Their wedding china was colorful botanic ware hand-painted with different varieties of flowers and vegetables. She ordered bright orange moreen bed hangings and she loved vivid roses, poppies, and pink honeysuckle. She wanted a beautiful landscape.

Reuben, in contrast, saw the garden as an extension of his major interests—natural history and agriculture. "He was as proud..." Lloyd wrote:

...of his cabbages, fruit trees, and Glycene Apios (ground nut) as he was of the many rose bushes he and Jane planted. Besides his general interest in the cultivation of the earth, Reuben was an avid student of natural history and a close friend of such early 19th century naturalists as Thomas Nuttall, Thomas Say, Rubens Peale and his brothers Franklin and Titian, and John James Audubon. Sometimes alone and sometimes accompanied by one or more of these friends, Reuben traveled through the countryside collecting unusual plant specimens which he then pressed and incorporated within his herbarium, still housed at Wyck. Similarly, he swapped seeds and cuttings with friends in Germantown and with acquaintances from New England to the Deep South.

Reuben also appreciated the use of nature as an educational tool, especially for his own children. He wrote a very tender letter to Jane about this in 1818.

…with what pleasure will I not welcome thee to the scene of my present interesting occupations, put under thy tender charge the garden and see thy taste displayed in every shrub, and in the light festoons of every vine trace the hand that gave them grace. With what additional pleasure will I not aid thee in imparting instruction to our daughter and after the daily task has been cheerfully performed lead her forth into the garden and the field & teach her to admire the economy of vegetation in the bursting forth of the pumula and radioles of the legumes her little hands have deposited in the earth, point out the bees as examples to stimulate her industry, and see our mantle decked with the wild flowers which she has assisted to gather. But this picture impresses too deeply the privations thy absence occasions to thy attached friend and Husband

Their daughter and subsequent family members who lived at Wyck learned their lessons and loved the place. They updated it with lush Victorian plantings and made it more refined during the colonial revival period, and today a conscious restoration is underway to return the garden to the Reuben-Jane period without destroying valuable specimens added later.

As Sandra MacKenzie Lloyd wrote:

In Reuben's eyes, it was essential that parents teach their children to nurture the earth and make it fertile with vegetables and flowers. His philosophy corresponded with Quaker beliefs that the earth was a gift from God to man. Man, then, had the responsibility and pleasure of cultivating the earth for his own benefit and as a celebration of God's goodness. These tenets and their application to daily life helped make Quaker Philadelphia a center for agricultural and horticultural achievements during the eighteenth and nineteenth centuries.

The Pennsylvania German tradition was elaborated upon when Reuben Haines maintained extensive vegetable gardens and cropland at Wyck. The calm horticultural beauty of Jane Bowne was more Quaker-inspired. Beauty and utility: Quaker and Dutch.

The pioneer Pennsylvania German public garden re-creations are at the Landis Valley Village and Farm Museum. The most striking of these four square gardens is shown as part of the Log Farm complex, which concentrates on interpreting eighteenth-century farm life. The overall view taken from a "cherry picker" is like a schematic illustration of the garden form.

Never as elaborate as the gardens at Wyck, there were almost certainly gardens on the property of what is now the Landis Valley Village and Farm Museum since the mid-eighteenth century. The museum has been a pioneer in the revival of the traditional Pennsylvania German garden, and it is also home to the Heirloom Seed Project, which makes traditional Pennsylvania Dutch varieties of vegetables and flower seeds widely available. The image of actual historic gardens at Landis Valley is blurred. Gardens by their very nature are transient. Those with little in the way of substantial structure leave few traces, especially in land that has been disturbed over many years.

Henry Landis's diary is of great value. The diary has many references to digging the garden or "Emma's garden," for his wife Caroline Emma Landis (1842–1929), Henry was occasionally the digger, but the work was more commonly done by a hired man: "Billy is digging garden," [April 10, 1889]. Henry wrote on a fine warm Saturday day in April 1881, "…I dug garden, I finished two large beds, the boys hauled in the manure." There are also frequent references to whitewashing the fence: "Geo whitewashed the garden fence on the inside" [April 17, 1881]. Pales for garden fencing were also mentioned on a regular basis. For example, Henry and "the boys" went to Lancaster on April 27, 1876, where among his other purchases were "a Keg of nails and some 300 four foot pails [sic] from B. B. Martin." Elsewhere he values pales at two cents each.

While the Landis Valley Village and Farm Museum founders, George Diller (1867–1954) and Henry Kinzer Landis (1865–1955), collected some garden-related tools and implements they never consciously recognized the garden itself as an artifact to be preserved. In their lifetime it was just, perhaps, too commonplace.

The only known document about the gardens at Landis Valley as a museum in the brothers' day looks like this:

List of Herbs
Landis Valley Village and Farm Museum Herb Garden
Planted by the
MENS GARDEN CLUB
Of Lancaster
Compiled by Mrs. Walter F. Kaufman

And it bears a stamp:

Landis Valley Museum
H. K. Landis
Geo. D. Landis
LANCASTER
PA

The garden planted under the brothers' supervision near the reconstructed tavern building was a colonial revival herb garden with thirty-seven varieties of plants ranging alphabetically from Angelica to Woodruff, and including elecampane and gas plant, along with the more expected mints, tansy, and sage.

Each entry in "The List of Herbs" is keyed, describing plant usage: "a annual b biennial p perennial attractive to bees CU Chief use in medicine and cooking today according to the findings of the Brooklyn Botanic Garden m medicinec culinary."

Among the very un-Dutch information we are given is that "Roman Wormwood" is used in making "Vermouth" and that chamomile is good for flavoring sherry!

The most unusual inclusion on the list is:

Helleborus niger. Black Hellebore. Christmas Rose. Rare even in the old herb gardens. It was classed with the strewing herbs. In the garden it was usually planted near the house because it was believed that not evil spirit would enter a dwelling near which these plants were grown. It is a perennial of very long life. It is not uncommon to have a clump over thirty years old. Always difficult to grow in this region there is no Christmas Rose on the property today.

The most elaborate entry was devoted to Rosemary:

Rosemary. Rosmarinus officinalis. P * Not hardy here. Wood shrub, beautiful narrow green leaves. Tiny bright blue flowers. Spicy nutmeg odor. Warm balsam taste. According to old writers this plant is full of virtues—its leaves placed under the bed prevent the sleeper from having evil dreams; its flowers placed among clothes and books prevent moths from destroying; if the leaves are boiled in white wine and the face and brows washed therewith "thou shalt have a faire face"; and the odor of a box made of the wood of rosemary was said to preserve youth. In mediaeval times Rosemary was used as a garland on the most important dish at festive occasions [sic]. The leaves are used by the Italians today for flavoring. CU c A strewing herb, garnish and for flavoring.

Note the information that the herb is used "… by the Italians today for flavoring." It certainly is not a staple of Dutch cookery. Rosemary today is grown in the Heirloom Seed Project's display garden.

George and Henry's spiritual heirs, the Landis Valley Associates and the Curators of Landis Valley Village and Farm Museum, have remedied the Landis gardening lapse and the grounds are dotted with appropriate gardens. We would hope that the Landises would find at least some of them familiar.

Periodically the entire wooden structure of the garden boards lining the beds, as well as the fence, need to be replaced. This is the best time to study the structure of the garden—and how it is put together.

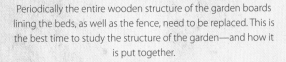

The wooden elements—the boards and the fence—color up very quickly.

The Pennsylvania Germans didn't compost, but they fed weeds and excess vegetation to the pigs, which were traditionally housed in styes convenient to the garden. Pig manure was favored in vegetable gardens. Landis Valley's pigs are heritage breeds.

Volunteers help prepare the garden in spring.

The garden paths are of packed earth, now covered with wood chip mulch.

Watering was traditionally done with an oak bucket.

Onions thrive next to a harvesting board.

Costumed interpreters cultivate and harvest crops.

Geese not only eat bugs in a garden, they are excellent "watch dogs," and sound an alarm when strangers approach.

The four square garden and its perimeter at the Brick Farm at Landis Valley is planted with a variety of vegetables, herbs, and flowers and represents the gardens of the first half of the nineteenth century.

Julia Child visits Landis Valley Museum

Meets with Pa. German food expert and author, William Woys Weaver

By Steve Keplinger
Sunday News Staff Writer

It's not every day that The French Chef meets an expert on Pennsylvania German cuisine in country surroundings reminiscent of England.

Yet that's what happened recently when Julia Child, one of the most famous names in food, visited with cookbook author William Woys Weaver in the gardens of the Landis Valley Museum to tape a segment of ABC's "Good Morning America."

The segment, due to air this week, served a double purpose: to introduce Child, known best for her 1970s Public Broadcasting Service series "The French Chef," to the delights of area cooking as detailed in Weaver's book "Pennsylvania Dutch Country Cooking" and to note the success of the museum's Heirloom Seed Project, which encourages the preservation of historic fruits, vegetables and grains.

Despite a canceled flight which delayed her arrival, Child maintained a gracious air and genuine interest as Weaver and museum curator of agriculture Steve Miller escorted her through the buildings and gardens of Landis Valley. They were followed by a camera crew and a handful of delighted museumgoers snapping photographs. Not at all shy about enjoying her surroundings, Child at one point happily munched a juicy Red Brandywine tomato during the shoot.

"It looks a little bit like England," Child said later, admiring the green surroundings of the Garden Spot.

■ Weaver's ties to the area and Child's interest complemented the segment's focus on the museum's Heirloom Seed Project, which cura-

Page G-16 — JULIA

Sunday News/Jack Leonard
Julia Child and author William Woys Weaver talk food as they enjoy the garden that is part of Landis Valley Museum's Heirloom Seed Project.

The gardens at Landis Valley have even attracted celebrities.

A contemporary private four square garden in Lancaster County, Pennsylvania, emphasizes flowers over vegetables and another features topiary in the center. *Lee Stoltzfus.*

A four square garden at the splendid privately owned German-Georgian house, "Charming Forge," is purely ornamental in scale.
Lee Stoltzfus.

Some German gardens were built on terraced, rather than flat, ground. Portions of this garden appear to be on more than one level. An apple orchard is at the right.
Mr. and Mrs. Michael B. Emery Collection.

Left, top to bottom | A beautifully maintained Victorian era farmhouse in Montgomery County, Pennsylvania, has traditional outbuildings and a four square garden lined in stones and boards. The grape arbor is also a feature found in or near many Pennsylvania German gardens.

The Amish of the Great Valley near Bellville in Centre County, Pennsylvania, have evolved their own variant of the four square garden, employing concrete. Their center bed often features flowers, and an elevated birdhouse.
Continued on page 86. | *Lee Stoltzfus.*

The self-propelled tiller and cultivator sounded the death knell for many traditional gardens. *Landis Valley Village and Farm Museum Collection.*

In addition to the vegetable or kitchen garden many farms featured a truck patch, or *die Lott,* which produced large quantities of staples and vegetables for market. The Landis Valley version of die Lott are the growing fields for the Heirloom Seed Project, which is plowed and fertilized using animal power.

Protecting young bean plants in die Lott.

As the years went on, and the use of the rototiller proceeded, a new Anglo-German garden emerged, planted in rows, and often featuring a row of flowers. This one is next to the Stone Tavern complex at the Landis Valley Village and Farm Museum.

A common presence in die Lott, chickens eat bugs and grubs, but they also scratch, which can injure young plants.

A woman hoes an unfenced truck patch, or die Lott, on a modest farm. The small Germanic stone end-chimney house form was familiar in Berks County, Pennsylvania. Note the grape arbor attached to the house. It provided fruit as well as a pleasant shady area where the housewife could work on a sunny day. A smokehouse is to the right. This impressionist painting was done by Ralph D. Dunkelberger (1894–1955). *Schwarz Gallery, Philadelphia.*

Cabbage grows in another truck patch near a farmhouse complex, as shown in an anonymous painting, circa 1890. *The Cottage Collection.*

OTHER PENNSYLVANIA HERITAGE GARDENS

Evolving after George and Henry's day is a Pennsylvania German Garden that is especially popular with Amish and some Old Order Mennonites. Often called a "runway garden" or a "ribbon garden," it is linear and parallels an extensive vegetable garden or, occasionally, the road front of a cornfield. A distinguishing feature of the runway garden is the limited number of plant varieties it contains. Usually no more than three varieties of annuals are used, but one or two kinds are common. As you ride through rural Lancaster County today, if you see a linear bed of purple petunias and orange marigolds, twenty-five or fifty-feet or more long, you can be almost certain you are looking at a Plain farm.

In addition to private gardens, there have also been some large-scale ornamental gardens developed by German church and sectarian organizations. The most extensive and longest lasting were created by the Moravians, who also provided early America with several important botanists.

The Moravians are a Protestant denomination founded in the eighteenth century, but one that traces its roots to the *Unitas Fratrum* (Unity of Brethren) Hussite movement in fifteenth-century Bohemia and Moravia. Surviving as an underground movement, "the hidden seed" was brought into public notice through the efforts of Count Nikolaus Ludwig von Zinzindorf (1700–1760), when a group of families following the traditions of the Bohemian Brethren fled Moravia in 1722 and settled on the Count's estate in Saxony. On von Zinzindorf's land, they founded the Village of Herrnhut, which would become the mother community of this group, and one that attracted Pietists from all over Germany. Central to this group was a lasting evangelical zeal and soon after the move to Herrnhut the first foreign missionaries were sent out to minister to black slaves in the West Indies. Within twenty years missions were in places as varied as South Africa, Greenland, Surinam, and North America.

The pioneer Moravians in the thirteen original colonies began their work in Georgia in 1735 where Zinzindorf saw an opportunity to evangelize the Indians and to create a haven. Unsuccessful there, the group turned to Pennsylvania in 1740 where they quickly founded Bethlehem and Nazareth. A few years later, Lititz followed. The Moravians also relished the prospect of uniting Pennsylvania's German settlers—Lutheran, Reformed, or sectarian—in a union church. The effort ultimately failed, but during von Zinzindorf's fourteen-month American stay (1741–1743) he did succeed in establishing the Moravian church in the New World.

Moravians from Pennsylvania founded Salem, North Carolina, in 1753. Moravian communities, whether in Pennsylvania, North Carolina, or elsewhere, were carefully planned and developed. They often featured ornamental communal gardens open to the community and widely praised by visitors. This story has been detailed in James Murtagh's *Moravian Architecture and Town Planning in America*. The Moravians began as communitarians, with their society divided into "choirs," or groups, by age, marital status, and sex, where all lands and industries were owned by the society. This system would dissolve and privatization was the rule by the end of the eighteenth century. However, until the mid-nineteenth century, the successful Moravian communities were closed to all but Moravian residents. Today, the historic portions of their major American centers function as combination church-owned facilities, schools, and museums.

Old Salem, the museum area that now preserves surviving portions of the Moravian settlement Salem, has a very active garden program, which preserves and recreates historic gardens and builds on the Moravian tradition of providing public gardens and park space.

Strawberry plants grow next to a raised bed in early spring on an Amish farm in Lancaster County. *Lee Stoltzfus.*

Cold frames are permanent features in front of this Lancaster County, Mennonite home. *Lee Stoltzfus.*

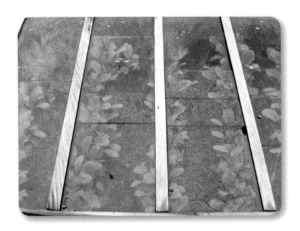

Cruciferous plants grow in a cold frame on an Amish farm. Another open cold frame displays an early lettuce crop. *Lee Stoltzfus*

Among the early Moravian botanists who had a great interest in native flora was Samuel Kramsch (1756–1824), who served for years at the Moravians' Nazareth Hall School in Nazareth, Pennsylvania. There he taught natural science to several important future Moravian botanists, including Christian Fredrick Denke (1775–1838) and Louis David von Schweinitz (1780–1834) before moving to North Carolina.

Not long after Kramsch arrived in Salem he wrote to Humphrey Marshall (1722–1801), a botanical mentor in Pennsylvania. "I botanized hereabouts," he noted, "as much as time would permit it, and found a great variety of plants between here and my former place [Nazareth], although much more difficulties concerning the heat, and especially the insects called Tiks [*sic*]."

Among the plants Kramsch found was the Carolina allspice (*Calycanthus Floridus*), which he described as exuding the fragrance of strawberries and growing very well in low-lying damp areas, "... especially near the mill." The allspice bush, with its sweet-smelling almost mahogany blossoms, became a favorite of the Pennsylvania German when it was introduced north, where it was often called "Sweet Smelling Shrub." Young girls liked to tie a blossom in a handkerchief to use as a sachet. It is probable that Kransch also introduced another Carolina native north, the Adam and Eve Plant, or the Lord's Candle (*Yucca filamentosa*), which would become so important in Pennsylvania German gardens.

Reused plastic buckets and plastic milk gallons, their bottoms cut out, are used to protect tender plants in early spring on Amish farms in Lancaster County. *Lee Stoltzfus.*

A runway or ribbon of tulips borders a Lancaster County garden.
Lee Stoltzfus.

Creeping Phlox (*Phlox subulata*) provide a flower runway next to a strawberry bed on the Elam Esh farm. Woods phlox
(*Phlox divaricata*) border the Christian Lapp Garden. *Lee Stoltzfus.*

The most important of the Moravian botanists was Louis David von Schweinitz, the Bethlehem-born grandson of Count von Zinzendorf. Christened "Ludwig," he anglicized his name early and on his scientific work he often signed his name with the less aristocratic "de" instead of "von." A missionary who held important posts in both Bethlehem and Salem, he botanized extensively for many years. His specialty was the study of fungi and his *Synopsis: Fungorum Carolinae Superioris* is the first important work published on American fungi and earned him the sobriquet "Father of American Mycology." Schweinitz's singular scientific work, *Synopsis: Fungorum in America Boreali*, which described 3,098 species, was published in the *Transactions of the American Philosophical Society* in 1832. Over his life he published almost 4,500 species of fungi of which more than 1,500 were believed to be new to science. From his work he was also able to establish ten genera. Additionally, he was interested in flowering plants and was especially attracted to the genera *Viola*, which includes violets and pansies. One of his best scientific papers is on the genus *Viola*, which in systemic botany is a very difficult genus because of its complexity. The research was published in the *American Journal of Science and Arts* in 1822. As a result of his interests he collected a large botanical library and he left a 23,000 species herbarium, now housed at the Pennsylvania Academy of the Natural Sciences in Philadelphia.

Another group with a rich garden-building heritage, but a more regional influence, was the Harmonists, who had broken from the Lutheran Church and had been badly persecuted in Europe.

For a retired farmer and his wife a simple tulip runway led to an obsession. The Weaver garden, alas, is no longer extant in southern Lancaster County. *Lee Stoltzfus.*

Runway or ribbon gardens are at their most glorious during the summer. All of these gardens are on Amish and Mennonite farms in Lancaster County. *Lee Stoltzfus.*

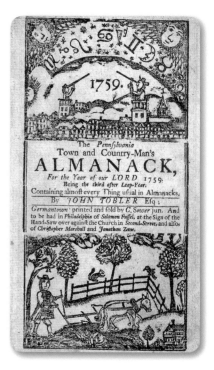

George Rapp (1757–1847), the son of a small farmer and vinedresser, gathered a group of 300 Pietist families who shared his beliefs. In 1803 Rapp, at age 46, sailed to Baltimore, Maryland, and subsequently bought 5,000 acres of virgin land just north of Pittsburgh, Pennsylvania. On July 4, 1804, about 300 of his followers arrived in Baltimore, followed by another 300 who landed in Philadelphia. In 1805, they formally united as the Harmony Society, and in their first year they built about fifty log houses, a gristmill, and a barn and workshops, and they started clearing land.

Harmony was soon to be prosperous, but it was inland from a navigable river and it was poor wine growing country. As a remedy, in 1814, the community bought 30,000 acres in Indiana's Wabash Valley, selling their original colony for $100,000. They also called their new settlement Harmony, which also prospered as more settlers joined them. In Indiana, however, malaria was rampant and their neighbors unpleasant. Accordingly, they sold the community to Robert Owen (1771–1858), the famed English reformer who established his famed New Harmony colony there.

Left | A young Amish woman harvests flowers in a floral truck garden. *Lee Stoltzfus.*

Center | The runway garden modified. A row of dahlias line a driveway leading to a garage in 1913. *The Cottage Collection.*

Right | Almanacs were of great importance to the Germans. They provided needed advice on planting times and festivals. Their covers and frontispieces were akin to trademarks. (Samuel?) Leach engraved the Almanac cover, with its farming vignette, for John Tobler's English language (but German oriented) *The Pennsylvania Town and Country-Man's Almanack*, published in Germantown by Christian Sower (Saur) II in 1759, *Winterthur Library, Printed Book and Periodical Collection.*

Now the community bought land at Economy, north of Pittsburgh, Pennsylvania, near their first settlement. By 1825, the entire community would be settled in their new town on the Ohio River where they would grow rich. A comfort-minded people, they were famous for their winery.

They were very enthusiastic practitioners of another Pennsylvania German tradition of growing carefully trained grapevines on the south-facing walls of their houses and many communal buildings. The fruitful deciduous vines shaded windows in summer and helped keep the buildings cooler by shielding masonry from direct sunlight.

The Harmonists were celibate and lived together in small groups constituting a "family." Each family house, in turn, had its own vegetable garden and adjoining the Great House, Rapp's House, there were elaborate ornamental gardens, rife with mystical symbolism and celebrated for their beauty.

Aesthetes, botanists, gardeners, or just plain folk, Pennsylvania Germans grew crops in a variant of the traditional four square garden, the most enduring of America's heritage gardens.

The Pennsylvania Germans have given American culture the Easter bunny and the decorated eggs—both of which are embedded in middle-European lore. The earliest known image of the Easter Rabbit in America is attributed to Conrad Gilbert (1734–1812) of Berks County. Images of baskets of eggs are extremely common as are highly imaginative Easter cards imported from Germany. The Pennsylvania Germans also introduced the Easter egg tree. Most elaborate was the "Easter Tree Putz," which belonged to the Gaumer family of Allentown, Pennsylvania. It contained more than 1,000 eggs and related items. Contemporary front yard displays replete with plastic eggs and bunnies are a common Dutch Country sight. *Easter Bunny, Abby Aldrich Rockefeller Folk Art Museum.*

Share the harvest. A traditionally minded gardener living in a modern Lancaster County homestead invites passersby to share the bounty.

Pumpkins in a farm wagon symbolize a season's end, as do canning jars to preserve the earth's bounty for winter.

III.

Visiting Gardens,

Garden Sites, and Heritage Landscapes

Wh
en, in the 1980s, co-author Irwin Richman began to lecture widely about Pennsylvania German gardens as a Commonwealth Speaker sponsored by the Pennsylvania Humanities Council, the audiences always included people whose parents or grandparents had traditional gardens. Some older folks remembered, with differing degrees of fondness, working in the gardens themselves. As the years went on, the audiences changed. Increasingly there was an interest in wanting to know how to create German gardens and where to see them.

Traditional gardens, tended by the traditionally trained gardeners, are moribund, but the Pennsylvania German four square garden is alive, well, and flourishing amongst hobbyists. Many gardens are tucked behind old houses, but a surprising number crop up in suburbia. The garden form is historic, yes, but it is also practical and adaptable to a small-scale property. Simply stated, a well-tended, raised- bed garden is extremely productive and environmentally friendly.

While books are a fine introduction and websites can provide additional pictures and information, nothing beats seeing actual examples of garden forms. Presented here is a list of Pennsylvania German gardens and related sites that are readily accessible. Rather than a simple alphabetical list, we have arranged sites by their educational and cultural interest. Because museum hours are subject to change, it is always wise to telephone or visit a website before visiting. Addresses, telephone numbers and websites, arranged alphabetically, are given in the appendix.

Happy touring—great learning is available everywhere.

GERMAN FOUR SQUARE GARDENS

The Landis Valley Village and Farm Museum is the first museum to interpret the Pennsylvania German raised- bed garden. The major demonstration garden is in the museum's Log Farm complex. In historic fashion, it is next to the pigsty where vegetable waste was tossed. Other raised-bed gardens are at the Brick Farm complex and the Stone Tavern and more German-influenced gardens are scattered over the site. The Museum's Heirloom Seed Project maintains a show garden of ornamentals and has gardens for raising seed crops. All are available for visiting. The museum also raises flax, corn and small grains, including wheat and rye, and has a small orchard of heirloom apples and period farm animals (cattle, horses, sheep, pigs and fowl—chickens, ducks, and geese) as well as historic barn types, period homes, and tool and farm equipment exhibits. More information on this site is elsewhere in the text.

Top left | A flax field.   *Top right* | Birdhouse gourds for sale.   *Center* | Harvesting rye.

Renfrew Museum and Park, Waynesboro, Pennsylvania

Maintained in cooperation with the museum by the Renfrew Institute for Cultural and Environmental Studies, this sixty-six-by-sixty-six-foot raised-bed garden was built in 2010–2011 and replaces an earlier garden at the museum, which was smaller and on a sloped site. Seen primarily as a teaching facility, the garden includes an astounding 300 varieties of plants (vegetables, herbs, and flowers) with nearby plantings of period-appropriate trees and shrubs. Located within Renfrew Park, a 107-acre holding left to the town of Waynesboro by its last private owners, the tract also includes the David Royer Farmstead, which is used to interpret life on a German farm, circa 1830–1870. There are appropriate farm outbuildings and the Visitors Center, housed in a large Victorian barn, displays farming and tanning tools, as well as one of the finest collections of pottery created by Pennsylvania German potter John Bell and his family. Also on exhibit is the only permanent display of artifacts related to Snow Hill Cloister, a nineteenth-century offshoot of the Ephrata Cloister that was (some buildings survive today) in nearby Quincy. Much of the landscape within Renfrew Park remains unchanged from the nineteenth century and has great period charm.

Renfrew Museum and Park

Historic Schaefferstown, Inc., Schaefferstown, Pennsylvania

Historic Schaefferstown has three major components: the circa 1758 Gemberling-Rex House, The Thomas E. Brendle Museum housed in a 1909 lodge hall built by the Patriotic Order Sons of America (POS of A), and the Alexander Schaeffer Farm, on which the four square garden stands. Alexander Schaeffer, the founder of Schaefferstown, acquired a 400-acre farm. The surviving tract of ninety acres comprises what is left of the farm today. The large four square garden, well-tended by dedicated volunteers, contains a wide variety of appropriate plants. The adjacent Schaeffer House was built circa 1758 and enlarged about 1771 by the builder's son Henry. An ongoing restoration, the house is especially noted for two whiskey still sites in the basement. The farm also has an eighteenth-century smokehouse and a period pigsty. The large bank barn was built in 1890 to replace an earlier structure that burned. While some modern incursions are visible, the site is large enough to give the visitor a sense of place in the eighteenth- to nineteenth-century Pennsylvania German landscape. The Gemberling Rex House located in Schaefferstown proper has varied plantings, including mature boxwoods, most reflective of the colonial revival period.

Schaeffer House

Historic Schaefferstown, Inc.

Frontier Culture Museum of Virginia, Staunton, Virginia

The original purpose of the museum was a historical interpretation of the "... intermingling [of] three principal ethnic groups—German, Scotch Irish, and English—on the frontiers of Pennsylvania, Maryland, Virginia, and the Carolinas. These groups pushed settlement into the interior after 1730, which resulted in the creation of a distinct American culture during the late eighteenth and early nineteenth centuries." Later, farmsteads depicting native American and African sites were added. For each culture group and in a subsequent "American Farm," whenever possible, period buildings have been moved to the site and placed in appropriate settings.

The German house and barn were moved to the site from the Palatine village of Hördt and the oldest portion bears the date 1688, although it was expanded later. The barn, a groundbarn or *grundscheier*, was built in 1727 and, like the house, is half-timbered or *fachtwerk*. Near the house is the kitchen garden in which time-appropriate vegetables, herbs, flowers, and berries are grown. Among the vegetables commonly cultivated were onions, peas, red cabbage, and kohlrabi. Gooseberries, currants, and elderberries were appreciated for fresh consumption and the making of wines and preserves. The Palatine Germans grew apple, plum, pear, and cherry trees, but commonly the trees lined a lane or were planted near a house rather than in orchards.

In the Palatinate, farmers lived in villages and rented, rather than owned, their lands, which was divided into the medieval three-field system with land holdings within walking distance of the village. The museum's house from Hördt stood originally on *Kirchstrasse* (Church Street) across from an Augustinian Cloister established in 1103. In the fields, crops raised in strips included cabbage, spelt (*triticum spelta*), and the American introduction, tobacco.

The Museum's "American Farm" is an admixture of German, Irish, and English cultures. Built from around 1835 through the 1850s by John Barger, of German descent, it stood in Botetourt County in the Great Valley [of Virginia]. One of the barns has a threshing floor and pens that are extremely similar to the one moved from the Palatinate. Vegetable gardening was practiced here but the four square garden has vanished. The buildings stood in the middle of their farm, which in its heyday raised grain (wheat and corn), cattle, and flax. To be able to see an Old World German farm and garden next to the Americanized counterpart is especially valuable.

Native American Farm. *Joe Schott.*

German Farm. *Joe Schott.*

English Garden. *Joe Schott.*

Peter Wentz Farmstead, Worcester, Pennsylvania

The centerpiece of the ninety-plus acre historic farm is the Peter Wentz House constructed in 1758, which combines English Georgian and Pennsylvania German architecture. The interiors are especially interesting for their extraordinary painted plaster walls, which have to be seen to be believed. George Washington actually slept here! He used the Wentz House as his campaign headquarters. It was here that he planned the Battle of Germantown and received word of the American victory at Saratoga. The garden fence is notable, made of rough planks (rather than pickets) with the boards spaced to allow air circulation. The four square garden re-creation is especially fine and well maintained and often contains plantings of complementary plants. For example, French marigolds (called "stinky flowers") are interplanted with beans to repel beetles.

In 1794 the property was sold to Melchior Schultz, a minister of the Schwenkfelders, a small German church well known for its members' prosperity, their needlework, and *fraktur*. It was during his period of ownership that Susanna Heebner painted an image based on the house and its garden. Descending in the Schultz family, the farm was sold to Montgomery County, Pennsylvania, which developed it as a center of colonial farming and re-created or restored the barn and other outbuildings.

Peter Wentz House in a field of mustard. *Peter Wentz Farmstead.*

Peter Wentz Farmstead.

Peter Wentz Farmstead.

1719 Hans Herr House, Willow Street, Pennsylvania

Built by Christian and Hannah Herr in 1710, this medieval-appearing Germanic stone house is also America's oldest surviving Mennonite meeting house. Preserved and restored by the Mennonite Historical Society, the house was constructed at a time when grain was especially valuable and often the difference between life and death. Grain was too precious to store in barns. Accordingly, this precious commodity was stored in the second level of the house's massive attic. The property has a large re-created four square garden and an orchard of period fruit trees. The grounds include several barns, a smoke house, a blacksmith shop, and a large collection of farm equipment from three centuries—eighteenth through early twentieth century.

A neighbor's mailbox
is the Hans Herr House
in miniature.

Ephrata Cloister, Ephrata, Pennsylvania

The Ephrata Cloister is a multibuilding complex constructed between 1735 and 1746 by the followers of Conrad Beissel (1691–1768), a charismatic German-born Protestant mystic. Within the Cloister were three orders: celibate men, celibate women, and married householders. After the society died out, the eighteen-acre site was sold to the Commonwealth of Pennsylvania early in the twentieth century and its eight buildings were restored by the Pennsylvania Historical and Museum Commission, which continues to operate the site today. The two surviving communal buildings, the *Saron* and the *Saal*, are unique in America for their early date, large scale, and medieval appearance. A nineteenth-century academy building is also on the site. The Ephrata Cloister was the center of extensive agriculture and garden culture. It was also a paper-making center. Its members were known for their *fraktur*, which often include images of nature. Examples of these illuminated manuscripts are on exhibit on the site. Ephrata was also a printing center where *The Martyr's Mirror*, the largest book ever printed in colonial America, was made. Largely vegetarian, the Cloister community originally had extensive gardens as well as grain, cabbage, bean, and flax fields. Today there are but two modest re-created four square gardens and one featuring dye stuffs rather than vegetables. The Cloister's beautiful park-like grounds give little idea about how the site was used in its heyday.

A costumed interpreter walks by the *Saron*. or Sisters House. *The Ephrata Cloister.*

A four square garden planted
with dyestuffs.
The Ephrata Cloister.

Hops.
The Ephrata Cloister.

The Golden Plough Tavern, General Horatio Gates House, York, Pennsylvania

The colonial complex, administered by the York Heritage Trust, includes a three-building grouping of The Golden Plough Tavern, The Horatio Gates House, and the Barnett Bobb Log House. Dating to 1741, the Golden Plough Tavern is a rare survival—a half-timbered Germanic structure within city limits. It is attached to the stone Georgian Gates House of 1751. The later Barnett Bob Log House was moved to the site. The re-created four square garden is a rare example of the form seen within an urban context and demonstrates the garden style's utility on a small lot. For the farm and garden-minded, the York Heritage Trust's Agricultural and Industrial Museum, several blocks away on West Princess Street, is also worth a visit. Housed in adaptively re-used industrial buildings, the complex displays agricultural artifacts used and/or manufactured in York County over a three-century period.

The Gates House (right) and the Plough Tavern. *York Heritage Trust.*

The Gates House (right) and the Plough Tavern. *York Heritage Trust.*

The York Agricultural Museum. *York Heritage Trust.*

Henry Antes Plantation, Perkiomenville, Pennsylvania

This is among the least-visited of four square garden sites. Virginia Smith, writing in the *Philadelphia Inquirer* in August 2011, observes, "... there is no crowd which is puzzling because this place … stirs ancient spirits and sooths twenty-first-century souls … and it is far less known than two other preserved Pennsylvania German homesteads —the Peter Wentz farm … and the Landis Valley Museum ..." The garden beds are defined, but not raised. Located in Montgomery County, Pennsylvania, the twenty-five-acre site is owned by the Goschenhoppen Historians, which are justly famed for their festivals, held on the grounds, celebrating Pennsylvania German culture and crafts.

In the colonial period, the term plantation simply meant a large farm producing crops for sale—and Henry Antes (1701–1755), the German–born builder, was both a successful entrepreneur and a man of affairs. A paper maker and a farmer, he was a Moravian convert active in religious affairs and he knew and worked with important Moravian leader Nicholas Von Zinzendorf and George Whitfield, a leading evangelist. Antes's great house, constructed in 1736, is amazing in that much of the interior is intact. Built with the traditional German three-room floor plan, the house also was the site of the first multicultural school in the American colonies. An outdoor bake oven stands near the re-created garden.

Henry Antes House.

An outdoor bake oven stands
near the kitchen door.

Gourds grow over the garden fence.

Quiet Valley Living Historical Farm, Stroudsburg, Pennsylvania

In the foothills of the Pocono Mountains, Quiet Valley is devoted to Pennsylvania German farming. The site has fourteen buildings ranging from 1765 to 1890, and emphasizes the life and family of Johann Zepper and his descendants who stayed on the farm from its founding in 1765 until 1914. Despite its name, Quiet Valley is a very lively place to visit with enthusiastic staff and farm animals and a wonderful four square garden and growing fields. The site has special events and classes throughout the year.

Quiet Valley Living Historical Farm.

An interpreter uses a grain cradle. *Quiet Valley Living Historical Farm.*

Schifferstadt Architectural Museum, Frederick, Maryland

The raised-bed garden at Schifferstadt is informative, the house is extraordinary, and the site houses a nice collection of agricultural implements. The 1758 house is a rare *dortganghaus*. Unlike most German houses of its period, Schifferstadt has a central hall with two of the rooms heated by stoves fed from the hallway. The house was built for German-born farmer Josef Brunner (or Brooner) who purchased a 303-acre tract that he named after *Klein Schifferstadt,* his hometown in the Palatinate, near Mannheim.

Schifferstadt Architectural Museum.

Schifferstadt Architectural Museum.

Wagner-Ritter House and Garden, Johnstown, Pennsylvania

Built around 1860, the Wagner-Ritter House tells the story of generations of immigrant steelworkers' families. It shows a rare example of a four square garden in a nineteenth-century urban setting, as well as a restored working class home. It is operated by the Johnstown Area Heritage Association and is a survivor of the disastrous Johnstown Flood of 1889.

Additional four square gardens are to be seen at several sites described in the following pages.

An urban backyard. *The Johnstown Area Heritage Association.*

Christ Lutheran Church (Long's Church), Stouchsburg, Pennsylvania.

THYME IN THE CEMETERY

A German garden tradition brought from the Palatinate is to plant creeping thyme (*Thymus serpyllun*) in cemeteries. As mourners visit the graves of their loved ones, a sweet pungent odor wafts up. This horticultural phenomenon can be observed, and inhaled, at numerous old graveyards. One of the best is in the older sections of the churchyard of Zion and St. John's Lutheran Church in Stouchsburg, Pennsylvania. The church's congregation dates to 1723. See more about Stouchsburg below. The cemetery of Falkner Swamp Reformed Church (now United Church of Christ) in Gilbertsville, whose congregation dates to 1725, also has a thyme-rich cemetery. An Americanism is the introduction of the Adam and Eve plant into the cemetery. It is shown here at Falkner and also in the Landis Valley Mennonite Church graveyard adjoining the Landis Valley Village and Farm Museum.

Drawn by folk artist Herman Markert,
circa 1880. *Jim Bohn.*

Early twentieth-century postcard.
The Cottage Collection.

Falkner Swamp churchyard.

Yucca in the Landis Valley Mennonite Church cemetery.

GERMANTOWN, PENNSYLVANIA, THE NEXUS

Few sites in our nation are more important to the history of American, and especially German, horticulture than Germantown, now a neighborhood of Philadelphia. Germantown was an independent community founded by Quaker and Mennonite families from Krefeld in modern Germany in 1683. Daniel Francis Pastorius (1651–1720), the group's leader and himself a gardener, developed a "… pretty little garden in which he grew … chiefly cordial stomachic and culinary herbs." Pastorius assembled America's first herbarium and authored the medical manuscript *Artznei buch*, a pharmacopoeia in which he emphasized herbs native to Pennsylvania. His house, much expanded, is privately owned and stands at 25 East High Street. Nearby, at 5253 Main Street, is the site of the home of Christopher Sauer (1721–1784), who published the first American herbal, *The Compendious Herbal*, which appeared in print between 1762 and 1778. A historical marker is at the site now occupied by Trinity Lutheran Church.

You can visit a significant garden site, Vernon Park, the story of which begins at the turn of the eighteenth century with one Matthias Kin, described in the *Pennsylvania Gazette* as "… an eccentric person who collects seeds …," who was sent to America by a group of German plantsmen to collect promising garden specimens. The local financial agent for the Germans was Melchior Meng, to whom Kin gave many plants, which Meng then planted around his Germantown home. After Meng's death, his twelve-acre homestead was soon acquired by Thomas Meehan (1826–1901), the great English-born plantsman. Later it became Vernon Park.

Daniel Francis Pastorius House. *Edwin C. Jellet, Germantown Gardens and Gardeners, 1914.*

In Germantown there are two significant Pennsylvania German gardens to visit:

Grumblethorpe, Germantown Ave., Philadelphia, Pennsylvania

Grumblethorpe, historically known as John Wister's Great House, was built in 1744 as a summer retreat by a Philadelphia merchant and wine importer and colorfully renamed by novelist Owen Wister (1860–1938). Behind the restored Germanic structure is an extraordinary garden area featuring a very impressive four square garden. Also in the garden is a splendid wisteria vine, appropriately so, since the plant was named for Dr. Caspar Wistar (1761–1818) by Thomas Nuttall. The Wüster family is descended from two German-born brothers who emigrated in the seventeenth century. One Anglicized his name to Wistar, one to Wister. In true German fashion, some family members intermarried creating Wistar-Wisters!

Grumblethorpe garden in 1914. *Jellet, Germantown Gardens and Gardeners, 1914.*

Wister's Great House and Tenant House (left). The blue and white sign is modern and obviously unavoidable. *Grumblethorpe.*

Grumblethorpe garden today. *Grumblethorpe,* Philadelphia.

Wisteria in bloom. *Lee Stoltzfus.*

Wyck, Germantown Ave., Philadelphia, Pennsylvania

Wyck is one of the oldest and best-documented gardens in America and is a melding of Pennsylvania German and Quaker cultures. The estate remained in single family ownership from the late seventeenth century until 1973 when it was opened as a museum. Originally a sixty-acre property, today it is a two and a half–acre site that includes a vegetable garden and fruit trees. Its most famed garden feature dates to the ownership period of Reuben Haines (1786–1843). Jane Bowne Haines sketched a "Plan of garden" in her garden notebook, 1821–1827, showing a four square rose garden. The garden as it appears today is both a preservation and a restoration bordered in boxwood. Many of the roses are descendants of Jane's plantings. The remaining grounds are planted in the English Romantic style. The house on the property is of great horticultural interest because it incorporates a conservatory developed when architect William Strickland enlarged the house in 1824. The property is described in greater detail in the preceding chapter.

The front of Wyck is set off by a tree-shaded lawn. Roses and clematis grow on the trellis on the house. Note the large potted plants brought out for the summer. In winter they are brought into the conservatory through the sliding glass doors at the center of the house, as designed by architect William Strickland in 1824. The photograph is one of a series of stereopticon photographs taken by local photographer Harry Lewis in 1871 or 1872. *Wyck, Philadelphia*

The Rose Garden. *Wyck, Philadelphia.*

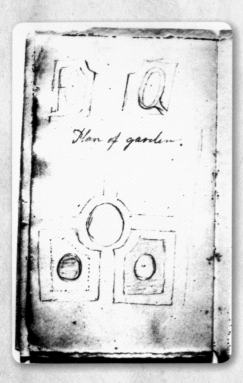

Jane Bowne Haines sketched her "Plan of garden" in her garden notebook, 1821–1827. It would become the basis of one of the oldest documented gardens in America, that at Wyck. It is essentially a four square garden where flowers, and especially roses, replace vegetables. *Wyck, Philadelphia.*

Fruits of the market garden. *Wyck, Philadelphia.*

Historic Rittenhouse Town, Philadelphia, Pennsylvania

Rittenhouse Town is a fascinating survival—an industrial and residential complex dating, in part, to the early eighteenth century. It was a center for paper making in America and was the birthplace of astronomer and clock and scientific instrument maker David Rittenhouse (1732–1796). The buildings all have a strong German vernacular cast. Alas, as Director Chris Owens laments, "I wish we had an authentic German garden, but we don't." The site, with its inter-relationship of structures in a landscape setting, is well worth the visit.

Historic Rittenhouse Town, an early cluster of industrial and residential buildings. *Historic Rittenhouse Town.*

Stenton, 18th Street and Windrim Avenue, Philadelphia, Pennsylvania

Stenton is an allied resource that anyone interested in gardens and visiting in the Germantown area should not miss. The home of James Logan (1674–1751), the house, built in 1730, is magnificently maintained by the National Society of the Colonial Dames of America. Logan interacted with his German scientific and farming neighbors. In the Renaissance tradition, he was a statesman (including being the chief justice of the Supreme Court and acting governor), a writer, a philosopher, and a scientist. His experiments to determine the sexuality of plants were praised by the great Linnaeus himself. His son, William, went on plant-collecting expeditions and built the still-existing orangerie about 1769, where he wintered and propagated tender plants. A descendent, John Caspar Wister, between 1910 and 1915, installed a colonial revival boxwood garden that is now being restored. A screen, entirely of native shrubs and trees, shields the house and grounds from the surroundings. It is very informative to compare the gardens and property to nearby Grumblethorpe and Wyck.

Stenton. *Stenton.*

The colonial revival garden. *Stenton*.

The Greenhouse. *Stenton*.

THE MORAVIANS

The Moravians are a Protestant denomination founded in the eighteenth century, but one that traces its roots to the *Unitas Fratrum* (Unity of Brethren) Hussite movement in fifteenth-century Bohemia and Moravia. Their history is outlined in chapter II, and today the historic portions of their major American centers function as combination church-owned facilities, schools, and museums.

Bethlehem, Pennsylvania

Bethlehem is the first and the grandest Moravian site in America and a stroll through the historic district is a wonder with its historic church, great commercial buildings, and well-preserved ambiance. Visit God's Acre, the cemetery with its flat gravestones, a distinctive eighteenth-century landscape feature. Museums to enhance your visit:

View of Bethlehem, 1754, engraved by Paul Sandby, shows extensive gardens. *Moravian Archives, Bethlehem.*

Central Moravian Church, Bethlehem, and a unique doorknob.

Moravian Museum of Bethlehem, Inc., Bethlehem, Pennsylvania

Housed in the 1741 *Gemeinhouse*, the largest log building surviving from colonial America, the museum houses many tools and textiles used by colonial-era Moravians.

Most of the impressive eighteenth-century Moravian buildings are set amidst colonial revival landscapes.

The eighteenth-century Schnitz House, so-called because historically it was used to prepare apples for drying and storage, is seen with Victorian plantings, including a circular flowerbed in an early twentieth-century view. In the 1970s, used as a home, it featured a vegetable garden. *The Cottage Collection.*

In God's Acre, Moravians were buried by choir group, rather than by family. Grave markers are equal in size and flat with the ground.

Behind façades on Church Street in Bethlehem are many attractive private gardens.

Colonial Industrial Quarter, Bethlehem, Pennsylvania

Among the extraordinary buildings in this site are the 1762 tile-roofed Waterworks and the 1761 Tannery. The site along the banks of the Monocacy Creek is picturesque and includes industrial ruins, including those of the Dye House.

The Colonial Industrial Quarter of Bethlehem along the Monocacy Creek is today set in a romantic landscape setting.

Burnside Plantation

The finest Moravian garden site in Pennsylvania is found outside of the historic core. This homestead of James Burnside and his family was an integral part of the Moravian farming system. The now-remaining six and a half acre tract is along the Monocacy Creek. The large farmhouse, summer kitchen, and two barns are interesting to see, but the large terraced raised-bed German garden is the star.

The house at Burnside Plantation.

Nazareth, Pennsylvania

Nazareth, Pennsylvania, is near Bethlehem and has significant architectural treasures. The historic district is part of the planned religious community laid out in the eighteenth century. Nazareth was a community closed to outsiders until 1858.

Old Nazareth, an 1854 watercolor by Rufus Grider. *Moravian Archives, Bethlehem.*

Moravian Historical Society, Nazareth, Pennsylvania

Housed in the 1741 Whitefield House, the museum's collection centers on items made and/or used by the Moravians. Its most important collection are the paintings by Johann Valentine Haidt (1700-1789), the premier eighteenth-century Moravian artist.

Whitefield House. *Moravian Historical Society.*

A Moravian log house. *Moravian Historical Society.*

Lititz, Pennsylvania

Lititz, Pennsylvania, located near the city of Lancaster, is the third major Moravian settlement in Pennsylvania. From its founding in 1755 until 1855, only Moravians could live in the town. Many homes and a large complex of church-owned eighteenth-century buildings survive, including the Sisters House and the Brothers House, located on Church Square. In the Moravian Church cemetery in the earliest quadrant dating from 1758, tombstones are flush with the ground. Linden Hall School, the second oldest girls' school in America, was opened in the Sisters House in 1746 and still is active today. The town's streets are tree-lined and private gardens abound. The most remarkable landscape feature is Lititz Springs Park, a private park owned by the Lititz Moravian Congregation and opened for public use.

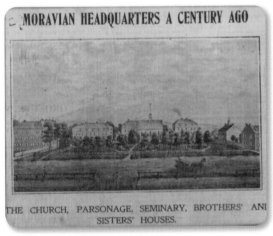

MORAVIAN HEADQUARTERS A CENTURY AGO

THE CHURCH, PARSONAGE, SEMINARY, BROTHERS' ANI SISTERS' HOUSES.

Church Square in Lititz, Pennsylvania, has many historic buildings including the small stone Corpse House, where bodies were kept prior to burial. The grounds themselves are landscaped in the English romantic style with touches of the colonial revival.

The entrance to God's Acre in Lititz, Pennsylvania, bears a legend reminding us that "The Dead Are Eternally With God."

God's Acre and a 1782 grave marker.

The Fourth of July. *Lititz Historical Society.*

Island and Fern Bed, Lititz Springs, Lititz, Pa.

G 6038   Lititz Springs, Lititz, Pa.   *Arrived here this morning*
Tommy

Lititz Springs Park, 1909 and 1911. *The Cottage Collection.*

A Lititz street scene.

A Pennsylvania German side porch garden.

A private garden in Lititz with an Old World feeling.

Lititz Historical Museum and The Johannes Mueller House, Lititz, Pennsylvania

The museum is devoted to Lititz history and the authentically furnished Johannes Mueller House, a 1792 log and stone house, is open for tours. Behind the society are the Mary Oehne Gardens featuring a Pennsylvania German four square garden and an ornamental water garden.

Old Salem Museums and Gardens, Winston-Salem, North Carolina

Of Moravian sites, Old Salem has the most period buildings you can visit and the most gardens. The buildings range in age from 1769 to 1861. Included among the gardens are the traditional one behind the Matthew and Henrietta Miksch House, built in 1771, the extensive Single Brothers garden, and a four square garden devoted solely to flowers at the John Siewers House of 1844.

Salem from the northwest, painted by an unknown artist, shows several gardens. *Private collection.*

The Matthew and Henrietta Mikish House, 1771.

Work in a garden is eternal. *Lee Stoltzfus.*

The re-created gardens of Salem are bountiful. *Old Salem, Winston Salem, North Carolina.*

The mid-nineteenth-century four square garden at the John Siewers House is devoted to flowers.
Old Salem, Winston-Salem, North Carolina.

Historic Bethabara Park, Winston-Salem, North Carolina

The site of the first Moravian settlement in North Carolina, its centerpiece is the recreated 1788 *Gemeinhaus*, which replaced a log structure built in 1755. The Krause Butner House of 1782 belonged to a potter. Landscaping is important to the site, which also includes a re-creation of the colonial- era stockade and the re-created Bethabara Hortus Medicus, the oldest well-documented American medical or physic garden, as well as the community gardens containing period plantings.

The re-created 1788 *Gemeinhaus* in Historic Bethabara Park. *Dennis Nodine.*

Bethabara Hortus Medicus. *Historic Bethabara Park. Gail Jones.*

THE HARMONY SOCIETY, AN AMERICAN ORIGINAL

The Harmonists were a sect that broke away from the Lutheran Church in their native Württemberg (Germany) and accordingly were persecuted. Their history is related in chapter II (see pages 93–97). Industry was important to them. They had a saw mill, a tannery, a woolen mill, a distillery, and an oil mill. They made their oil from poppy seeds they grew. They also raised grapes. English communal-scholar Mark Halloway observed in *Heavens on Earth: Utopian Communities in America, 1680–1880*:

> Rappites … liked to drink wine, and this may well be one reason why they appear to have been more mellow and human than some of their abstemious predecessors. They also enjoyed their food, and they did not stint themselves. Rising before five and six, they ate a light breakfast; at nine they lunched; at twelve they dined; at three they were ready for *vesper brodt*; between six and seven they rounded off the day with supper—and were in bed by nine.

They were famous for their winery and won awards for their silk. Halloway noted that the Duke of Saxe-Weimar, visiting Economy in 1826, only a year after its founding, was overwhelmed with enthusiasm:

> The warehouse was shown to us, where the articles made here for sale or use are preserved, and I admired the excellence of all. The articles for the use of the society are kept by themselves; as the members have no private possessions, and everything is in common, so must they, in relation to all their wants, be supplied from the common stock. The clothing and food they make use of is of the best quality. Of the latter, flour, salt, meat, and all long-keeping articles, are served out monthly; fresh meat, on the contrary, is distributed as soon as it is killed, according to the size of the family, etc. As every house has a garden, each family raises its own vegetables and some poultry, and each family has its own bake-oven. For such things as are not raised in Economy, there is a store provided, from which the members, with the knowledge of the directors, may purchase what is necessary, and the people of the vicinity may do the same.
>
> Mr. Rapp conducted us into the factory. … Their factories and workshops are warmed during the winter by means of pipes connected with the steam-engine. All the workmen, and especially the females, had very healthy complexions, and moved me deeply by the warm-hearted friendliness with which they saluted the elder Rapp. I was also much gratified to see vessels containing fresh sweet-scented flowers standing on all the machines. The neatness which universally reigns is in every respect worthy of praise.

The Rapps were a dynamic duo. Their successors were less able. "The success of the community was largely due to the combination of Father Rapp's spiritual leadership and with the remarkable administrative ability of his adopted son Frederich," noted Halloway. Millennialists as well as Pietists, the society began to decline after the death of George Rapp at the age of ninety. In 1807, the society had adopted celibacy, which also hastened its decline. The society, however, managed to last into the twentieth century. In the society's last years, it was controlled by the self-styled "Last Harmonist," John S. Duss (1860–1951), who used the society's accumulated wealth to the fullest, even to supporting and conducting his own symphony orchestra. The core of the carefully laid-out Germanic community, except for the church, is preserved and continually being restored by the Pennsylvania Historical and Museum Commission.

A statue of "Harmonie" is the centerpiece of the gardens. The Great House and the Church are in the background to the right.

Old Economy Village, Ambridge, Pennsylvania

This is a historic garden lover's paradise. In addition to several traditional family gardens, the sect's elaborate ornamental gardens, rife with mystical symbolism, have been reproduced centering around a garden pavilion housing a large painted wooden figure of "Harmonie." The garden also contains the Grotto, a rustic building with a neoclassic interior where persons were invited or compelled to go for contemplation. Also, on the Feast Hall and other buildings, grapevines are carefully trained.

A family garden.

The Grotto, set in the gardens, was a place of contemplation. Emblematic of the ideal human condition, it is humble in its exterior but beautiful within.

Grapes are trained on the south-facing wall of the Feast Hall.
Old Economy Village, The Pennsylvania Historical and Museum Commission.

Harmony Museum, Harmony, Pennsylvania

Contained in an 1809 warehouse and granary built by the Harmonists, the building is the center of a historical district including the village diamond, the Wagner House and Ziegler log house, the Harmonist Cemetery, and Father Rapp's Hillside Bench. Especially interesting as a remnant of Harmony Society landscape and valuable when combined with a visit to Old Economy.

Harmony Museum.

THE PENNSYLVANIA GERMAN LANDSCAPE

The Amish Countryside of Lancaster, Pennsylvania

A good place to start is the tourist destination of Intercourse, founded in 1754. The small roads and numbered highways that cut through the countryside are where you want to be, including North Hollander Drive, Ridge Road, and West Newport Road. Along these byways one sees many farmscapes and many "runway gardens," the typical Amish and Mennonite strip gardens bordering a vegetable garden or fronting a field. Other especially beautiful countrysides are in the Oley Valley and Great Valley.

Lancaster County countryside.

The Great Valley.

Along Amish Country roadsides. *Lee Stoltzfus.*

The Oley Valley in Berks County

The Oley Valley in Berks County is ten miles northeast of Reading, Pennsylvania, and includes all or parts of five townships, including Alsace, named for the German (now in France) homeland of many early settlers. The Valley retains a strong Germanic cast. While there are no homesteads regularly open to the public, several are owned by the Historic Preservation Trust of Berks County and can be visited by special arrangement, but there are many great Germanic farmsteads in this National Register Historic District. A least one privately owned historic building retains outlines of its historic garden. The Historic Preservation Trust's Keim Homestead is especially outstanding. The exterior can be visited every day.

Oley Valley.

The Fisher House from the back and its garden.

The Keim House.

Fisher House's ground barn.

The DeTurk House.

Millbach, Lebanon County, Pennsylvania

Millbach, Lebanon County, Pennsylvania, off state route 419, is completely "un-touristy" and a very fine example of a Pennsylvania German farm community, with a number of eighteenth- and nineteenth-century buildings. There are no restaurants or souvenir shops. The steeple of the Millbach Reformed Congregation (est. 1747) dominates the skyline. You can walk around the George Müller house circa 1752, now owned by a private foundation. A house and mill combination, part of its interior is on display in the Philadelphia Museum of Art.

Stouchsburg, Berks County

Stouchsburg, Berks County, is paralleled by State Route 422, which makes it possible to experience the layout of this one-time typical linear farm community built by the Pennsylvania Germans. Originally these communities had only one street. Houses were typically built close to the street with deep backyards that held gardens and a small barn. Drive or walk along Main Street then drive along Route 422 and see the backyards of all the houses on one side of the street. Nearby is Christ Church with its thyme enriched cemetery (see page 126).

A pigsty (now used for firewood) is attached to the building in the left background.

Top | View from Route 422.

Center | Four square garden behind the Black Dog Cafe.

Left | Gentrification comes to Stouchsburg in a pollarded fruit tree.

GARDENS WITH OTHER INFLUENCES

The next two sites have important Pennsylvania German connections with very interesting landscape treatments that are notable, but not in the Pennsylvania German tradition.

Conrad Weiser Homestead, Womelsdorf, Berks County, Pennsylvania.

German-born Conrad Weiser (1696–1760) was an important figure in colonial history. He was an advisor to the Penn family and an interpreter who knew several Indian languages. Additionally, he accompanied botanist John Bartram (see page 170) on an important plant-collecting expedition. He was one of the most prominent Pennsylvanians of his era. Weiser's principal home, long gone, was in Reading, but the Weiser Homestead was at the center of his original agricultural holdings, a tiny fraction (twenty-six acres) of which have come into public ownership. Leaders of the group overseeing the property wanted to landscape it properly. A local nurseryman was approached to create an appropriate scheme, which was subsequently shown to a prominent Reading textile millionnaire, who expressed his displeasure and offered to pay for a design scheme to be developed by the Boston, Massachusetts, architectural landscape firm Olmstead Brothers, founded in 1898 by two sons of Frederick Law Olmstead, designer of New York's Central Park. The subsequent design was completed under the supervision of Frederick Law Olmstead Jr. (1870–1957) and dedicated in 1928. The plan was never fully realized, and is not always well maintained, but it remains recognizable as an Olmstead creation—an improbable memorial to a Pennsylvania German pioneer and statesman.

The Weiser House (left) is eighteenth century. The large Sheetz House is later.
The Spring House supplied water for animals and the garden.

The monuments to Conrad Weiser and Chief Shikellamy are set in the Olmstead landscape.

Pennypacker Mills, Schwenksville, Pennsylvania

Samuel W. Pennypacker (1843–1916) was a lawyer, a collector of documents and artifacts, president of the Historical Society of Pennsylvania, governor of Pennsylvania (1903–1907), and intensely proud of his Pennsylvania German heritage. He was a direct descendant of Abraham Isacks op den Graeff (circa 1649–1731), one of the original settlers of Germantown (see pages 129–135). The house on the 170-acre farm-turned-estate was built in 1720, was purchased by Peter Pennypacker in 1747, and would remain in the family for eight generations before being acquired by Montgomery County, Pennsylvania.

In 1901, having decided to use the farm as a country estate, Samuel Pennypacker and his wife commissioned architect Arthur Brookie to transform and enlarge the old farmhouse into a stylish Georgian Revival mansion. At the same time they employed Thomas Meehan and Sons of Germantown to design the grounds. English-born, Thomas Meehan (1826–1901) owned what would become Vernon Park (see page 129). The Meehan firm was a pioneer in naturalistic landscaping—and the grounds remain as a wonderful example of an early twentieth-century style that remains stylish today, if not in the least Pennsylvania German. It reflects the cosmopolitan tastes of the heritage-proud yet culturally assimilated.

Pennypacker Mills.

Pennypacker Mills.

MORE HERITAGE GARDENS

Several historic gardens, while not German, have close alliances to the culture or have had a great influence on the heritage garden movement in America.

Bartram's Garden, Philadelphia, Pennsylvania

Bartram's Garden is the oldest surviving botanical garden in America and was home to John Bartram (1699–1777) and his son William Bartram (1739–1823), who are important in American gardening and botanical history. The garden was where plant explorers and botanists mixed. Conrad Weiser and other members of the German elite interested in "natural philosophy" visited and knew the Bartrams, including Louis David von Schweinitz (1780–1834) and members of the Muhlenberg, Wister, and Haines families. In 1765 John was appointed botanist to the king; John and William sent many American plants to England. John Bartram acquired the land in 1728 in Kingessing along the Schuylkill River, originally three miles from the city but now part of Philadelphia. The forty-four-acre property is especially known for its trees and is gradually being restored to its original straight-line schematic plantings.

Bottlebrush buckeye (*Aesculus parviflora*), left, and oakleaf hydrangea (*Hydrangea quercifolia*), right, grow in front of the Bartram House. Both, natives of the American Southeast, are Bartram introductions.

Franklinia altamaha, the Franklin Tree, blooms near the house.

Fothergilla major is named for John Bartram's English correspondent and patron, John Fothergill, MD (1712–1780).

Admiral de Constantinople, a parrot tulip, was introduced in 1665.
Bartram's Garden.

Colonial Williamsburg, Williamsburg, Virginia

This is where heritage gardening got its major impetus. Williamsburg gardens have become a trademark for the Anglo-Dutch garden traditions. Many of the gardens are ornamental and, perhaps, overly pretty, but several are of especial value for those interested in early kitchen gardens, and as a comparison to German gardens. The kitchen gardens at the Governor's Palace and the George Whythe House are especially recommended. To be mourned is the now-discontinued garden developed and shown briefly at Carter's Grove Plantation (see page 38).

Not everything is perfect in the gardens,
which are many and varied, including a naturalistic
interlude at the Governor's Palace.

Pennsbury Manor, Morrisville, Pennsylvania

This is the re-created country estate of William Penn developed from 1939 onward and is a spiritual descendent of Colonial Williamsburg. The gardens are in the Anglo-Dutch tradition and the kitchen garden is extensive. Penn was, of course, a rich man who employed trained gardeners, from England, at Pennsbury. We know the names of two: Ralph Smith (d. 1685) and Andrew Doz, whose children and grandchildren continued as gardeners at the estate. In 1685 William Penn's gardeners were growing many crops on the estate including:

> Kidney Beans and English Pease of several kinds, with English Roots, Turnapes, Carrots, Onions, Leeks, Radishes and Cabbidges. … Also I have such plenty of Pumpkins, Musmellons, Water Mellons, Sqwashes, Coshaws, Buck-hen, Cowcumbers and Sinnels of Divers kinds.

As at Williamsburg the gardens are great for comparison and contrast purposes.

Pennsbury Manor, The Pennsylvania Historical and Museum Commission.

Colonial Pennsylvania Plantation, Newtown Square, Pennsylvania

Embedded in the 2,490-acre former farmland comprising Ridley Creek State Park, the 112-acre Colonial Pennsylvania Plantation is a living history site dedicated to interpreting the period 1760 to 1790. The farm owned by the Quaker Pratt family was worked for over 250 years. On the land was an eighteenth-century farmhouse, a stone cabin, a spring house, and two barns. Since the Plantation's establishment in 1973 other buildings have been re-created, including a springhouse and a privy. The story told here is essentially of English Quaker farming and gardening. Given the scale, this is an excellent comparison study place to appreciate the similarities and differences between German and English Quaker farm and garden practices.

Colonial Pennsylvania Plantation.

Pennsylvania Hospital Physic Garden, Philadelphia, Pennsylvania

Philadelphia was an early center of medicine in the colonial and early federal period. Many doctors raised their own medicines and housewives, English and German, raised "simples" or medicinal plants. A physic garden was proposed for colonial Philadelphia to be modeled on London's famed Chelsea Physic Garden. A leader of the movement was Adam Kuhn, MD (1741–1817), born in Germantown and educated in Edinburgh, Scotland, and Uppsala, Sweden, where he was a student of Linnaeus. In 1768 he was appointed as first professor of botany and materia medica at the College of Philadelphia. In 1774 the managers of the Pennsylvania Hospital were petitioned to found an appropriate garden on the site. The garden did not come into being until 1976, the period of the American Bicentennial. Laid out along the traditional quadrant form, the garden contains many medicinal plants set in an attractive landscaped area.

Other garden/landscape sites are worthy of a visit. These represent Penn's Woods and are good study sites for the natural habitat that the Germans found—native trees, shrubs, and wildflowers.

Pennsylvania Hospital of the University of Pennsylvania.

Pennsylvania Hospital of the University of Pennsylvania.

Morris Arboretum of the University of Pennsylvania, Philadelphia, Pennsylvania

If you visit the gardens of Germantown (see pages 129–135), it is a short distance up Germantown Avenue to visit the Arboretum, developed upon the 175-acre estate known as Compton, owned by a remarkable brother and sister, scions of an Old Philadelphia family, John T. Morris (1847–1915) and Lydia T. Morris (1849–1932). While it has very sophisticated gardens, we draw special attention to the natural areas including the wetlands, meadows, and woodlands bordering the Wissahickon Creek. It is believed that some of the woodland has never been cleared and is a sliver of the original Penn's Woods.

The log cabin where Lydia Morris would serve tea to her guests in her natural garden.

Sculpture lurks
everywhere.

The only extant Edwardian fernery in America.

The Rose Garden.

The twenty-first-century Tree Top Adventure presents a unique view of Penn's Woods.
The Morris Arboretum of the University of Pennsylvania.

Bowman's Hill Wildflower Preserve, New Hope, Pennsylvania

Bowman's Hill was established in 1934 within Washington Crossing State Park. While the land has been timbered, a few notable historic trees survive. Today the preserve has nearly 1,000 of the 2,000 plant species native to Pennsylvania growing in naturalistic settings of woodlands, meadows, Pidcock Creek, and a pond. The Preserve can be explored on two and a half miles of walking trails. Many wildflowers are also propagated on site. Sale of these native plants are part of the Preserve's mission.

An Eastern tiger swallowtail butterfly (*Papilio glaucus*) feasts on a milkweed (*Asclepias*).

Left | Yellow lady's slipper (*Cypripedium parviflorum*). *Bowman's Hill Wildflower Preserve.*

Mt. Cuba Center, Hockessin, Delaware

In 1935 Pamela and Lammot duPont Copeland built a stately colonial revival house near the village of Mt. Cuba, on one of the highest points in Delaware. The site was chosen because Mrs. Copeland, a native of New England, was homesick for rolling hills. While originally a traditional estate with formal gardens laid out by Marian Coffin, the Copelands (especially Pamela) became increasingly interested in native plants, especially those of the Piedmont of the eastern United States. Today fifty acres of wildflower gardens and 550 acres are "managed as our Natural Lands." A staff of thirty-six professionals tends to the place and the spring wildflower bloom is extraordinary. In the fall, the spot is a favorite for foliage watchers and those who like late-blooming wildflowers.

Mt. Cuba Center.

Monticello, Charlottesville, Virginia

In a category all by itself is Monticello. Always being upgraded and restored, the gardens were designed by Thomas Jefferson to be what is characterized as "… a botanic laboratory of ornamental and useful plants from around the world." In Monticello's 1,000-foot-long garden terrace, Jefferson grew 330 vegetable varieties, including seeds of varieties he had received through William Bartram and other Pennsylvania sources. If it grew in southeastern Pennsylvania, it probably could be grown at Monticello, and many of the plants mentioned in this book can be found growing (and identified) in this unique garden. A recent book by longtime garden director Peter J. Hatch, *A Rich Spot of Earth! Thomas Jefferson's Revolutionary Garden at Monticello*, details it all. Jefferson's gardens are, in many ways, the *summa* of what was grown in our Eastern gardens.

IV.

Heirloom Seeds

Seed bags used by traditional Pennsylvania German seed savers. *Collection of Clarke Hess.*

An impossible array of heirloom flowers grown from bulbs are seen as a cutout mounted in a vintage album. *The Cottage Collection.*

Before the age of hybridization offering the newest of everything, humor was often used to sell seeds. J. M. Philips, founded in 1872, is still in business although not owned by the original family.

The genesis of the modern seeds, those commonly sold in colorful packages, is succinctly explained in Sue Strickland's book, *Heirloom Vegetables*:

…For millennia, farmers and gardeners were the plant breeders, improving crops by selection from generation to generation. In the 19th century, rather than waiting for changes to occur at random in nature, a few experimenters started to make deliberate crosses between plants. By choosing the plants carefully, these early hybridizers hoped that the offspring would have the desirable characteristics of both parents. …

In fact, these are often the plants we cherish as "heirloom seeds." Then the tale becomes more complex.

At first new varieties were developed by individuals and small family-based seedsmen, still with the involvement of farmers and gardeners, but techniques gradually became more sophisticated. There were also pressures to make plants of the same variety less variable, so those with slightly "wrong" characteristics (for commercial purposes) were weeded out. Over several generations varieties were developed that were very uniform and reproduced that uniformity; these were known as "pure lines." In the 1930s the first F1 hybrid corn varieties were produced, the seed coming from crossing two inbred pure lines. F1 hybrids of other crops soon followed.

The emphasis would shift from the growing fields to the laboratory.

In the last 25 years [from 1998], plant breeding has become the specialist realm of microbiologists, geneticists and other scientists. It is a complex major industry. Dozens of potato varieties, for example, can be screened for blight resistance in the glasshouse within 3–4 weeks of germination, rather than growing them in a field for several months, and any useful material resulting can be held in test tubes using tissue culture. Genetic engineering allows specific genes in plants to be located and marked in the laboratory, and then moved between species in a way that was never possible with traditional hybridization methods.

The results have been profound and, for many, alienating.

Today farmers and gardeners are seldom involved in plant development. It is geared to the perceived needs of industry, which is typically concerned with relatively short-term gain. Plant breeding has also become extremely expensive: for example, the development and marketing of one of the first genetically engineered varieties to be released, the Flavr Savr tomato …, is said to have cost in excess of 95 million US dollars. With such investment, it is no wonder that a few varieties dominate the shelves of superstores, and the pages of catalogs.

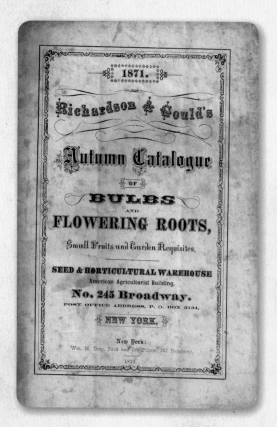

Seed catalogs in the post-Civil War years evolved from simple informative booklets to those with showy, eye-catching colorful covers. Plants newly introduced from Asia were especially popular.

Mr. and Mrs. Michael B. Emery and The Cottage Collection.

Europe and the British Isles were the source of most seeds sold in early America. Because of long sea voyages, supplies were uncertain, quality varied widely, and seeds tended to be costly. In March 1797, for example, Hannah Marshall Haines, an avid Quaker gardener in Germantown near Philadelphia, lamented that new flower seeds were "too expensive to buy," as reported in *Germantown Green*.

Seeds were offered for sale through advertisements in newspapers. One of the first of these is found in the February 1719 edition of the *Boston Gazette*:

Garden Seeds.—Fresh Garden Seeds of all Sorts, lately imported from London, to be sold by Evan Davies, Gardener, at his house over against the Powder House in Boston; As also English Sparrow-grass Roots, Carnation Layers, Dutch Gooseberry and Current bushes.

One Richard Francis appears to have been in the seed-selling business for a number of years. A brief advertisement for his wares appeared in the *Boston Gazette* in 1737. Eleven years later, an advertisement in the *Boston News-Letter* (March 3, 1748) lists an impressive selection of seeds:

Garden Seeds.—To be Sold, by Richard Francis, Gardner, living at the sign of the black and white Harre at the South end of Boston, fresh and new imported in the last ships from London, all sorts of Garden Seeds, as follows: Windsor, Sandwich, and Hotspur Beans; long Hotspur Ormats, & Hotspur Pease; early Dutch Cabbages; Battersy, Sugar-loaf, large Cabbages; Imperial, Silesia, brown Dutch, & curl'd lettice; orange and yellow Carrots; early Dutch Turnips; green & yellow turnips; smooth & long Parsnips; white, Spanish, Strasburg, & Welsh Onions; London Leek; Short-top London, & Sandwich Reddishes; round-leaf spineges; Collley-flowers; ende (endive) sallet; sweet Marjoram; Thyme; Summer Savory; Hyssop; Sage; Balm; Dubet; Parsley; & Parsley Dubet; Pepper-grass; & single white mustard; Cucumbers; Musmellon; Watermellons; and all sorts of the best flower Seeds.

An advertisement in the *Maryland Journal and Baltimore Daily Advertiser* on March 8, 1793, is even more extensive —and also offers nursery stock imported from the Old World.

Maximilian Henisler; Nursery Man and Seeds Man, at his Plantation, on the Main Road to Philadelphia, about a Mile and a Quarter from Baltimore-Town, begs Leave to inform the Public, that he has now on Hand, and fit for Sale, A Variety of Kitchen-Garden and Flower Seeds of the best kinds, and such as can be depended on, viz: Cauliflower Seeds; Roman Brocoli; Cabbage of different Sorts; savoys ditto; Dutch Kale of various Colours; Scotch ditto; German Greens; Hanover Turnips; double Parsley; round Spinach; red English Carrot; the large French carrot; the early Horn Carrot; Parsnips; white Mustard; early Windsor Beans, early Bunch Beans, large Dutch Caseknife Bean, The Lima Bean, The French speckled Bean, the white French Kidney Bean, the small white French running ditto; early Peas; Bunch Peas, Marrowfat Peas, the French Sugar Pea; the early white and red Radish, fit for Hotbeds, the Turnip Radish, Scarlet Radish, Salmon ditto, Common Radish, Summer Radish, the large white and black Winter Radish; Cabbage Lettuce of various sorts, long Roman Lettuce Seed; curled Endive, broad-leafed ditto; Succory variegated; Tongue Grass' Pepper Grass; Leek Seed, red-top Turnips; French celery, Dutch Headed Celery; the

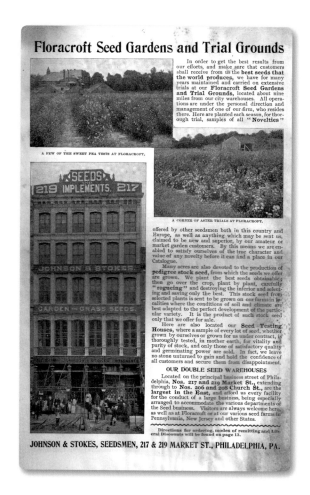

Floracroft Seed Gardens and Trial Grounds

In order to get the best results from our efforts, and make sure that customers shall receive from us the **best seeds that the world produces**, we have for many years maintained and carried on extensive trials at our **Floracroft Seed Gardens and Trial Grounds**, located about nine miles from our city warehouses. All operations are under the personal direction and management of one of our firm, who resides there. Here are planted each season, for thorough trial, samples of all "**Novelties**"

A FEW OF THE SWEET PEA TESTS AT FLORACROFT.

A CORNER OF ASTER TRIALS AT FLORACROFT.

offered by other seedsmen both in this country and Europe, as well as anything which may be sent us, claimed to be new and superior, by our amateur or market garden customers. By this means we are enabled to satisfy ourselves of the true character and value of any novelty before it can find a place in our Catalogue.

Many acres are also devoted to the production of **pedigree stock seed**, from which the seeds we offer are grown. We plant the best seeds obtainable, then go over the crop, plant by plant, carefully "**rogueing**" and destroying the inferior and selecting and saving only the best. This stock seed from selected plants is sent to be grown on our farms in localities where the conditions of soil and climate are best adapted to the perfect development of the particular variety. It is the product of such stock seed only that we offer for sale.

Here are also located our **Seed-Testing Houses**, where a sample of every lot of seed, whether grown by ourselves or grown for us under contract, is thoroughly tested, in mother earth, for vitality and purity of stock, and only those of satisfactory quality and germinating power are sold. In fact, we leave no stone unturned to gain and hold the confidence of all customers and secure them from disappointment.

OUR DOUBLE SEED WAREHOUSES

Located on the principal business street of Philadelphia, **Nos. 217 and 219 Market St.**, extending through to **Nos. 206 and 208 Church St.**, are the **largest in the East**, and afford us every facility for the conduct of a large business, being especially arranged to accommodate the various departments of the Seed business. Visitors are always welcome here, as well as at Floracroft or at our various seed farms in Pennsylvania, New Jersey and other States.

Directions for ordering, modes of remitting and Liberal Discounts will be found on page 13.

JOHNSON & STOKES, SEEDSMEN, 217 & 219 MARKET ST., PHILADELPHIA, PA.

French small Soup Turnip; the Dutch white and yellow Turnip; the Roman Thistle; Artichoke; broad-leafed Basilic common ditto; small leaf ditto; an Assortment of Musk Melons, and Cantaloupe ditto, of the best kind; green Cucumber, large Spanish white Cucumber; Asparagus Plants of the best Sort; an Assortment of Flower Seeds, too tedious to mention; double Tuberose Roots; finer and larger than any imported; a large Quantity of different Sorts of Vines, viz: Burgundy, Rhenish, Tokey, Madeira, Muscat, Claret, the Provence or Coast Vine.

He has just received from Europe, A large and general assortment of Bulbous Roots; and expects a Quantity of choice Fruit-Trees, which, when arrived, shall be publicly advertised.

While some American-grown seeds were produced for sale in the late eighteenth or early nineteenth century our available information about individuals is spotty at best, although we know of the career of Grant Thorburn (1773–1863), a Scotsman who produced seeds in New York under the name of "Grant Thorburn, Seedsman and Florist." But it was the remarkable religious group the Shakers who really established the American seed industry. The Shaker faith was created by an English woman, Mother Ann Lee (1736–1784), who seated the first group of her followers in New Lebanon, New York, in 1776. The Shakers, communitarian and celibate, were extremely active in attracting new members. In the 1850s, at their most successful, there were fifty-six Shaker settlements in the United States —with most in New York State and New England.

Seeds had become a big business by the second half of the nineteenth century but most merchandise was essentially heirloom stock. At the Floracroft Trial Grounds, they tested novelties and "... anything which may be sent to us claimed to be new and superior, by our amateur or market garden customers," i.e. natural selections, rather than man-developed hybrids.

To support themselves, the communities farmed and engaged in the manufacture of simple, well-made items including furniture and baskets. Using meat and dairy in moderation meant that their gardens and orchards were prime necessities. Many Shaker communities also sold their excess vegetables and fruits. The business of growing seeds had begun as early as 1780 and was in full swing by 1800. Most of the seeds were grown in Hancock, Massachusetts, and in Watervliet and New Lebanon, New York. Other communities produced lesser amounts.

Some Shaker seeds were of unusual varieties and, to the modern eye, were put to surprising uses as reported by a Shaker sister in *Good Housekeeping* magazine in July 1906:

> We always had extensive poppy beds and early in the morning, before the sun had risen, the white-capped sisters could be seen stooping among the scarlet blossoms to slit those pods from which the petals had just fallen. Again after sundown they came out with little knives to scrape off the dried juice. This crude opium was sold at a large price and its production was one of the most lucrative as well as the most picturesque of our industries.

The **opium poppy** (*Papaver somniferum*), as author Michael Pollan describes it, is "...a tall breathtaking poppy, with silky scarlet petals and a black heart...." While seeds for this heirloom are widely available, technically growing this genuine heirloom can be considered a felony under state and federal law, although the plant is now a wilding in many areas.

Early on, Shaker seeds were sold by the bushel, the scoop, or by weight, as was the custom with farmers, but some time around 1812 the Shakers came up with the idea of putting smaller quantities of seeds in packets, a practice that would become universal. Shaker wagons went from village to village leaving seeds to be sold at small town stores at a twenty-five percent commission. Unsold seeds were collected from stores during the summer. Shaker seeds became the standard for reliability and annual sales were in many thousands of dollars. The business continued until 1890.

Many other growers had entered the trade and it was this competition, together with the decline of the number of the celibate Shakers, that led to the religious group's closure of their seedhouses. By the post-Civil War years large-scale commercial growers were sending out tens of thousands of seed catalogs, many adorned with full-color front covers made possible by the low cost of large volume chromolithography and favorable postage rates.

David Landreth and Sons of Philadelphia, founded in Philadelphia in 1784 and still in existence today, albeit in rural Sharon Springs, New York, is generally considered to be the first truly successful commercial seed house in America. Landreth was an important grower of seeds of plants brought back by the Lewis and Clark expedition, especially the Osage Orange (*Maclura pomifera*), which was widely planted as hedges throughout America. Landreth was also one of the first seed companies to import and grow seed varieties from Japan when that country opened itself to trade with the West in 1853. As early as 1811, Landreth produced catalogs.

B.K. Bliss and Sons of New York City is believed to have introduced mail-order marketing to the seed business and it is also the first known company to include color plates in their seed catalogs, which they did starting in 1853. The period 1860 to 1900 is considered the golden age of chromolithography as applied to catalogs. After that time photography and photographic reproduction gradually replaced chromolithography and the photographer replaced the commercial artist as the source of most catalog illustrations. Commercial artists continued to work well into the twentieth century illustrating many seed-related publications. In the twenty-first century, we are experiencing the return of artists, as a market has emerged for old-fashioned or heirloom seeds. Quaint-looking catalog covers and seed packages work best when created with the

By the late nineteenth century most farmers bought most of their seeds.

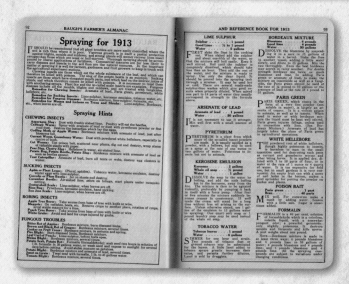

Large scale commercial food production required (and still requires) heavy-duty pest control.
In more innocent years, arsenic was an especially favored insecticide.

hand of the artist—often replicating the feel of the chromolith or the delicate hand of polite lady painters. Catalogs with colorful covers clearly became the norm; however, many catalogs continued, as they continue today, to be produced in black and white. Usually this was a matter of economy, but today plant specialists often prefer black and white catalogs to emphasize that theirs is an elite and special clientele that first, does not need bold images to attract them, and second, that knows what the specialty plants look like.

While many hundreds of thousands or even millions of seed catalogs were distributed by stores, salesmen, and via mail during the golden age of chromolithography, relatively few survive. Many were cut up for pretty pictures to be put in albums or simply tacked up on a wall. Many catalogs saved by people who thought they were too good to throw away were then tossed out by the people's heirs. Most have just disappeared. Those that survived are treasured by a number of repositories, including the Landis Valley Village and Farm Museum in Lancaster, Pennsylvania, the Library of the University of Delaware, The National Agricultural Library and, of course, the Smithsonian Institution, which is aptly called "America's Attic."

Seed packages are even less likely to survive, although "America's Attic" has preserved a number as well. The original Shaker seed packages were simply small top-opening envelopes with hand-written inscriptions, and most seed packages remained simple, with printing replacing hand script—perhaps with the addition of an engraved black and white illustration.

As the scale of the seed business grew and concepts of marketing changed, so did seed packages. The industrial scale of the new seed companies is beautifully illustrated in a series of engravings and photo engravings included in the 1882 *Seed Annual* produced by D. M. Ferry and Company of Detroit, which features a massive warehouse and illustrations of workers raising, processing, and packing seeds. Founded as Gardner, Ferry and Church in 1856, following the retirement of Misters Gardner and Church in 1879, the firm was incorporated as D. M. Ferry and Company. In 1930 the company merged with the C. C. Morse Company of California to become The Ferry-Morse Company. In 1959, the business relocated its home garden division to western Kentucky, chosen because it is at the junction of several major rail lines, making it an excellent distribution point for North American operations. In 1981 Ferry-Morse became part of an international conglomerate, France's Groupe Limagrain, which claims to be the largest breeder-producer of horticultural seed worldwide. Today Ferry Morse, as the modernized company is known, uses the slogan, "The Hand That Seeds The World."

Seeds ordered from seed catalogs with bright colors could be shipped in utilitarian packets, but changes were in the wind. In traditional retail stores most merchandise was behind a counter—the customer requested it. Patrons shopping for seeds were no different. Customers would ask for what they wanted and be handed a packet of seeds. Forward-looking merchants like F. W. Woolworth recognized the value of making low-cost goods easily available and relying on impulse-buying to help boost sales. In the seed business this meant the development of the bright eye-catching seed package and the racks in which to display them.

D. M. Ferry and Company again was one of the first companies to employ brightly colored seed packages. Its founder Dexter Mason Ferry (1833–1907), born in Lowville, New York, is usually credited with inventing the "commission box," which is the seed rack commonly used for retail display. Like many of his generation, Ferry was highly moralistic and had an almost missionary zeal for his product. In the centennial edition of the *Seed Annual*, in 1876, Ferry proclaimed, "Ladies should cultivate flowers as an invigorating and inspiring outdoor occupation. Many are pining and dying from monotony and depression, who might bury their cares by planting a few seeds …" Vegetable gardening was promoted as fine out-of-doors exercise for men. Working outside would also "… develop that attachment of the citizen to his home, which is one of the strongest safeguard of society against lawlessness and immorality."

By the early years of the twentieth century racks of these bright eye-catching seed packages were found in general stores everywhere and soon in many of the specialty shops that emerged: hardware stores, grocery stores, gas stations, as well as Mr. Woolworth's five-and-dime stores. A few of these early seed packages were hand-tinted lithographs, but these were soon driven out by chromolithographic packets derived from artists' renditions. These were followed by photoengraved color illustrations by the 1920s, which might be either artist created or photographic. These were followed by frankly photographic images, especially after World War II. Contrary to the old adage "Photographs don't lie," photographers and photo processors can, and often do. Photographic images have always, and they continue today, to be enhanced to improve the perfection ratio and color intensity of their subjects. In the world of seed package photography, insect and weather damage do not exist. Flowers and vegetables are at their peak or in bud. They are images of perfection. As with catalogs in the twenty-first century, with the continuing popularity of wild flowers and heirloom vegetables and flowers, artist-created fantasy images mimicking the antique styles have become very popular.

Reflecting and/or leading in all major trends in catalog and seed package design over the years is W. Atlee Burpee and Company of Warminster, Pennsylvania. Founded in the American centennial year, 1876, by Quaker W. Atlee Burpee (1858–1915), the firm, which originally grew all its seeds at their Fordhook Farms in Bucks County, remain famed for their Fordhook Hybrids, synonymous with the latest in plant hybridization. Following more recent trends, the catalog also features heirloom varieties side by side with the "latest" and "newest" introductions. Along with other catalogs, Burpee's reflects another modern trend—offering fewer varieties of each vegetable or flower than did earlier editions.

W. Atlee Burpee, like his older competitor, Dexter Mason Ferry, believed fiercely in the efficacy of gardening and producing high-quality seed. He passed this passion on to his son and grandson, who ran the company for many years and were well known in garden circles, especially for their quest for a pure white marigold.

In 1970 David Burpee sold the family company to General Foods for $10,000,000, which, in turn, sold the company to IT&T. When plans to expand the brand did not progress as envisioned, the company, its identity tarnished, returned to private hands. Now under the presidency of George Ball, Burpee is continuing to regain much of its popularity as the producer of what it touts as "Gardening's Most Wanted Catalog." Other companies certainly might dispute this claim. In the gardening year 2003–2004 with a new, mostly empty, office, co-author Irwin Richman decided to amass *all* the garden catalogs that came to his home and office. They made a stack almost two feet high. Working on this book, he and Mike Emery have amassed an even larger stack.

By the twentieth century most farmers and gardeners, in Pennsylvania and nationally, were buying their seeds and proud of their use of hybrids—this even among many of the Plain people. After Amish farmer Joseph F. Beiler's death, early this century, he was eulogized for his piety and his traditional ways, but as a farmer, within community restraints, he was as progressive as he could be. "He was one of the first to use a field chopper to cut hay, blow it onto a wagon, and haul the feed to the cows. [and] New seeds and county agents' recommendations all caught his attention," wrote Samuel Stoltzfus.

While modern seeds are very well adapted to commercial production, many hybrids give their best yields only under ideal conditions. Additionally, many modern hybrids were deficient in both taste and aroma or scent compared to traditional varieties—which were soon almost completely unavailable, unless you personally knew a seed saver. Beginning in the 1960s, orchardists and gardeners began to realize that thousands of varieties of fruits, vegetables, and flowers were disappearing. We were not only losing their special qualities, but their precious genetic material was slipping away. Monocultures were becoming manifold and genetic diversity was in danger of being lost.

The modern heirloom seed movement can be dated to 1975 with the founding of the Seed Savers Exchange by Diane and Ken Whealy. Since then the interest in yesterday's foods and plant varieties have gone mainstream. Very dramatically, many Americans turned away from the perfect round red tomato to the rainbow of heirloom hues. *Johnny's Select Seeds.*

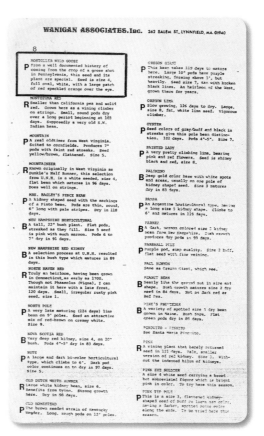

Wanigan Associates, devoted to heirloom beans, was founded in the 1980s by John E. Withee (1910–1993).
Lee Stoltzfus.

Many people were concerned about this. Kent and Diane Whealy became the most successful of people to do something about the situation. In 1972 Diane Whealy's grandfather Ott entrusted to his granddaughter and her husband the seed of three plants that his forbears had brought from Bavaria to northeastern Iowa generations before. "These were two vegetables—a large German tomato and a prolific climbing bean—and a beautiful dark strain of the flower Morning Glory."

Soon after Grandpa Otto's death, Kent Whealy recalls in a foreward to Sue Strickland's *Heirloom Vegetables*:

Diane and I immediately started trying to locate other families who were also keeping heirloom seeds, hoping to increase the genetic diversity available to gardeners growing healthy food for their families (43 million US families, about 40%, grow some part of their own food, and two-thirds of the world's people live on what they can grow). We soon discovered a vast, almost unknown genetic treasure quietly being maintained by elderly gardeners and farmers. Heirloom seeds are especially prevalent in isolated mountainous areas, such as the Ozarks, Smokies, and Appalachians, and also among traditional peoples such as the Mennonites, Amish and Native Americans. It became immediately apparent that these were excelled home garden varieties, often extremely flavorful, tender, and productive. Gardeners are continuously growing and comparing varieties: those that don't measure up are

Early efforts were directed to preserve seeds grown by Native Americans. *Lee Stoltzfus.*

Heirloom seed pioneer Lee Stoltzfus stands beside a bean teepee he built in his Lititz, Pennsylvania, garden in the 1980s. *Lee Stoltzfus.*

quickly discarded, certainly not maintained for 150 years or more. And over such long periods, many of these heirloom seeds had slowly developed resistances to local diseases and insects, and had gradually become well adapted to specific climates and soil conditions. This heritage of heirloom seeds, which vastly outnumbers the offerings of the entire garden seed industry in North America, had never been systematically collected.

Diane and I founded the Seed Savers Exchange in 1975. For more than two decades we have continued to locate gardeners keeping heirloom food crops, and have organized them into an annual seed exchange. Each January SSE publishes a yearbook that lists all of the seeds being offered by our members. In 1975 that network consisted of 29 members offering a few dozen varieties through a six-page newsletter, now there are 1,000 "listed members" offering nearly 12,000 rare varieties through the current 400-page *Seed Savers Yearbook* sent to 8,000 gardeners. Over the years SSE's members have distributed an estimated 750,000 samples of rare seeds that were unavailable commercially and were often on the verge of extinction.

Today there are organizations devoted to seed saving in various countries, and the heirloom seed phenomenon developed as many forces came together: a search for heritage, the quest for healthier foods, a widespread rejection of corporate culture and the homogeneity it fosters, and the maturity of living history museums. The Seed Saver movement has remained a touchstone for many individuals and organizations and its influence and help was instrumental in the founding of what would become the Heirloom Seed Project of the Landis Valley Village and Farm Museum— the first

program devoted to preserving and documenting Pennsylvania German seedstock. It was through The Seed Savers Exchange in Decorah, Iowa, that a young gardener living in Lititz, Pennsylvania, obtained most of his earliest historic seeds in the 1980s, although he had also gotten some from Lancaster County neighbors. Lee Stoltzfus, a photographer is also, he says, "a backyard gardener by avocation and a garden designer by trade … one generation removed from the Amish horses and plows." Lee relates in "Elements of a Four-Square Garden" in *Kitchen Garden Magazine*, "For my Amish grandparents, gardening meant survival. It meant food for the table during February snow storms … and food for a household of nine children and assorted in-laws. It was not a weekend pastime or an evening's recreation." For Lee, growing heirloom plants connected him with a past that he cherished, although he was no longer Amish himself. Special impetus for his interest came when his friend, Clarke Hess, bought an eighteenth century Lititz homestead, which had been built by Clarke's many times great grandfather in the early 1700s. Lee and his brother Larry landscaped it and Lee created the four square garden.

Curious and meticulous, he would trace seeds from Seed Savers that had local connections to their source, which led him to interesting tradition-minded farmers, including Daniel Brubaker of Ephrata who was locally celebrated for his fruits, nuts, and vegetables. Brubaker introduced Lee to other growers who, along with his combing of local fairs and farmers markets, enabled him to find over a dozen varieties of antique seeds. At a Lancaster farmers market, for example, he found Groff's Lazy Wife Beans, a pre-1810 strain, and two Morgantown women provided him with Fisher's Old Woman Beans and Lutz Beets, both pre-1900. And, while Lee prefers to find his seeds locally, this was not always possible. He found the Gnuttle Bean in the large Amish community of Holmes County, Ohio. "Gnuttle," he relates in a letter in his archives, "is Pennsylvania Dutch for red, speckled, cutshort." He had to go further for "his most important find … a seed corn called Lancaster Surecrop, which was developed by Isaac Hershey of Lancaster County." Lee noted that it "… was one of the three most important corns used to develop modern hybrids." Further, "It's a major contribution of Lancaster County to American agriculture." His sources were seed collectors Carl and Karen Barnes from Turpin, Oklahoma, who found it in Oklahoma City.

The more involved Lee became with heirloom seeds and heritage gardens, the more he realized that he needed an institutional connection for his program to thrive. A museum would be ideal and he knew that within the profession there were already sources for historically correct apple varieties and period-appropriate animal types. He turned to the nearby Landis Valley Village and Farm Museum, especially to Stephen S. Miller. Like Lee, Steve was then in his twenties. Steve was the farm manager then; he would later become the museum's director.

Steve was very concerned about the plants being grown in the Landis Valley gardens. One of his duties was to show the gardens to visitors, who were increasingly asking questions about the gardens' historical authenticity: "Was this how the gardens looked?" and "Are these the plants the Dutch grew?" Steve found himself giving increasingly complex answers. "The garden form was right … but the seeds often came from the Burpee catalog." This was fine for the home gardener, but certainly not ideal for the museum.

When Lee approached Steve the time was right for all of the pieces to fall into place. Steve called it, "… a marriage made in heaven." The museum could improve its gardens and in Lee gained an advocate possessed with a store of knowledge and a hobbyist's zeal. Among the other early volunteers who helped develop what became the Heirloom Seed Project was Nancy Pippert, a registered nurse by profession, who had a talent for establishing the records and databases needed for the program that developed around heirloom seeds. A dedicated gardener, she also worked in the gardens, first as a volunteer, then as a part-time employee of the Landis Valley Associates. She was, indeed, a "founding mother" of the Heirloom Seed Project.

Together Lee, Steve, Nancy, and others worked to persuade the administration of the Landis Valley Village and Farm Museum and the Pennsylvania Historical and Museum Commission to establish the pioneering Heirloom Seed Project (HSP). Publicity helped launch and establish the program. The *Lancaster New Era* ran not only articles about it but also a major editorial in support. A few years later a two-page spread about the new program appeared in the *Philadelphia Inquirer*, which was subsequently picked up by many of the other Knight-Ridder newspapers nationally. Hundreds, or perhaps thousands, of letters came from the many German-settled areas all over America—some offering support, others wanting to order seeds. Founded in 1985, the project celebrated its 25th anniversary in 2010. While the HSP enjoys official recognition from the Commonwealth, it receives no state funds; rather it is supported by the Landis Valley Associates and the work of about fifty volunteers who care for the gardens and prepare and market the seeds, which has been done through catalogs, seed lists, and now, increasingly, on the Internet and by direct sales at the Landis Valley Village and Farm Museum Store, which is also operated by the Landis Valley Associates.

Starting on a shoestring, the new project's budget didn't even allow for padded mailing envelopes. After complaints from customers about crushed seeds, toilet paper and paper towel tubes were ingeniously used as effective mailing protectors. Accordingly, the HSP started a collection. Museum volunteers Ray and Evelyn Althouse, wintering in Florida, would put up a notice in their winter home community and arrive at Landis Valley each spring with a station wagon full of tubes—until the need subsided.

An important and popular fund raiser for the HSP is the annual Herb and Garden Faire held each May, for which volunteers raise thousands of seedlings for sale from the heirloom seed collection. The event has grown to become the largest of its class in the East and today features "… more than 90 vendors … with herbs, historic seeds, and garden accoutrements," as a 2014 promotional poster for the event noted. Each winter project director Joe Schott offers a very popular tree grafting course featuring scions from the Landis Valley Village and Farm Museum's collection of historic apple varieties. The course has also

Steve Miller, founder of the Heirloom Seed Project at the Landis Valley Village and Farm Museum, is shown in the Log Farm's raised-bed garden in 1985. With him is Nancy Pippert, the site's garden coordinator.

The volunteers who make the Landis Valley Heirloom Seed Project possible pose on the porch of the 1848 Landis Valley Hotel.

The Seed House where seeds are processed, packed, and shipped. The house has since been repainted but the autumn scene is glorious.

developed into a regional scion exchange where collectors from neighboring states, as well as Pennsylvania, come together to exchange starts of historic varieties as they learn and practice the physical techniques of grafting.

By mission, the Landis Valley Heirloom Seed project "… preserves seed varieties having historical significance to the Pennsylvania Germans between the mid-1700s and 1940." The whole project, as suggested earlier, is made possible by determined volunteers who, with professional supervision, "… work with as much accuracy as possible to present precise information about our seeds, plant varieties and historical gardening techniques," as noted in the Landis Valley seed catalog in 2005. Additional information was provided in the annual catalogs the HSP distributed. These small sales booklets were also educational. While the catalogs have been replaced by plant lists, there remains an almost religious zeal about the project's goals, as this excerpt from a catalog shows:

One of the most frequently asked questions is how do we come upon our historical information. [Lee Stolzfus's experiences are amplified.] Local research is the first step to determining the "age" of a variety. Local research consists of people and the information that they share. Our varieties have come to us with stories of "seeing this in my grandma's garden" or "my great-grandmother brought the seeds for this plant from Germany when she and my great-grandfather immigrated." We listen for physical descriptions of the seeds, plants and fruits so that when we "trial" these varieties in our experimental gardens, we have characteristics to look for and are watchful for consistencies season after season.

Diaries, old seed catalogs and almanacs, newspapers and magazines are some of the other areas that we explore in the name of research. We work with other preservationists such as William Woys Weaver, author of *Heirloom Vegetable Gardening* and Seed Savers Exchange to assist in our documentation process. Without the cooperation, sharing and common goals of other preservationists, the Heirloom Seed Project and other organizations like us could not exist.

The Heirloom Seed Project is not only a link to our past, but also to our future. Without non-hybrid seeds, such as those the Heirloom Seed Project strives to preserve, commercial seed companies and researchers could

A very new Heirloom Seed Project showed part of their modest production at Landis Valley's
Harvest Days in the mid-1980s. *Lee Stoltzfus.*

What is the difference between heirlooms and modern hybrids?
Landis Valley staff member Beth Leensvaart's signs give the simple answer.

not develop the hybrid varieties that "feed the world." Without the open pollinated varieties that we offer, many people would not know the heritage that is theirs to enjoy. Without organizations like the Heirloom Seed Project, many of our "antique" varieties would be lost forever to future generations.

In growing heirloom seeds, care must be taken to prevent inadvertent cross pollination which, of course, produces hybrids, of often unknown parentage. Heirloom gardeners who grow more than one variety of a particular vegetable and want to save their own seeds must be cognizant of the ways in which these plants pollinate. This "Cross Pollination Chart" is adapted from the one published in the Heirloom Seed Project Catalogs.

Before seeds are ready to be identified as Heirloom Seeds for sale, the project's workers always grow several generations of the plants, always carefully rogueing the plants…something home gardeners who are also seed savers must do. As HSP materials explain:

Rogueing is the process of going into the garden, going through the plants and removing any that are not true to type in order to keep the variety pure. …. It is important to do this from early in the growing season right through fruiting. Ideally, plants which are showing "off traits" can be removed (rogued) before they flower and fruit to prevent unwanted cross-pollination.

In order to rogue out the plants you don't want, you have to know what to look for at various stages in a plant's life. You can gather this knowledge from books on heirloom plants or by experience. You can remove any variety that does not follow your expectations in plant size, blossom color, fruit set and size, taste, color, and so on.

Occasionally, fluxes in environmental conditions such as weather and soil can affect the size or production of fruit. It will not affect blossom color, leaf shape or fruit shape. For example, if a tomato should be round and it appears oblong, or if a purple bean is green with white stripes, you probably have a problem!

Beans are among the easier plants to rogue out. We've noticed that some older bush bean varieties throw runners now and then. They don't remain compact like bush beans usually do. With some of these older varieties, that type of vining may be part of their background, especially if everything else is all right with the bean. However, if the runners are really long and you get the distinct impression that your plant is turning into a vine rather than a bush type, it is probably best to pull those plants. When you're walking through a planting of beans, look for obviously stunted plants or those that are growing overzealously, as well as pods that are the wrong shape, size, or color. These are the ones you'll want to rogue out.

VARIETY	WILL CROSS WITH
Beans *Leguminosae Family*	Perfect flowers; self-pollinating but may occasionally be crossed by honeybees and other insects. Crossing varies depending on type of flower, population of insects, etc.
Beets *Chenopodiaceae Family*	Wind pollinated; beet pollen is very light and can travel up to five miles. **All beets and chard will cross with each other.**
Carrots *Umbelliferae Family*	Insect pollinated. **All carrots will cross with each other and with Queen Anne's Lace** (*wild carrot*).
Chard, Swiss *Chenopodiaceae Family*	See beets; will cross with all chard varieties and all beet varieties
Kale *Brassicaccae Family*	Most kale and all collards will cross with all other members of *B. Oleracea* including cabbage, broccoli, brussels sprouts, cauliflower, and kohlrabi.
Lettuce *Compositae Family*	Bee and insect pollinates; will cross with other lettuces including wild. Some dispute degree of crossing.
Melons *Cucurbitaceae Family*	All varieties of *cucumic melo* will cross but will not cross with watermelon or other cucurbits.
Tomatoes *Solanaceae Family*	In dispute,
Radishes *Brassicaccae Family*	Insect pollinated and will cross with all varieties of wild and domesticated radishes. They will not cross with any other members of *Brassicaceae Family*
Rutabagas *Brassicaceae Family*	Self-futile: capable of self pollination. May be cross-pollinated by insect if different varieties grown with 1 mile of each other; Will also cross with some agricultural turnips, or Fodder Turnips, and with all varieties of Winter Rape.
Spinach *Chenopodiaceae Family*	Wind pollinated; very light pollen.
Orach *Mountain Spinach*	Wind pollinated; Very light pollen.
Turnips *Brassicaccae Family* *Brassica rapa*	Will cross with each other and Chinese cabbages, Chinese mustard, and broccoli raab. They will not cross with any other Brassica species/
Gourds *Cucurbitacae Family*	Cross with gourds and zucchini.
Cucumbers *Cucurbitaceae Family*	All cukes will cross with each other.

SEPARATION ISOLATION METHODS

Separate white seeded varieties. Use tall interplantings to separate varieties. May use cages for bush plants. May use blossom bags for climbers,

For absolute purity, isolate by 2–5 miles. Bag or cage (Min. 6 beets per cage or bag)

Isolate by ½ mile. Hand-pollination and caging.

See beets.

Grow only one variety of *B. Oleracea* per season, or isolate by one mile or cage.

25 feet separation of varieties. Caging ensures seed purity. Just before flowers open, wrap seed heads with spun polyester or put cage in place.Remove cage when plants stop flowering and begin to dry.

Isolation; caging with introduced pollinators. Hand pollination. Grow one variety per year.

Cage or separate by 100 feet.

Separate varieties by ½ mile or cage; protect from wild population by removing plants.

Separate by 1 mile or cage

Grow one variety per year or bag.
(Spinach plants male or female; plant large plantings closely in wide beds for good ratio.)

Grow one variety per year or bag.
(Spinach plants male or female; plant large plantings closely in wide beds for good ratio.)

Isolate different varieties by 1 mile.

Isolate varieties by ¼ to ½ mile; hand pollinate if grown close together.

Isolate varieties by ½ mile or hand pollinate.

The Herb and Garden Faire is always held on the Friday and Saturday just before Mother's Day.
With about ninety vendors, it attracts regional buyers who enjoy the plants, the ambiance, and the help
and information from the project's volunteers.

Techniques of harvesting seeds vary from variety to variety. Mostly this is a simple process that just requires patience, vigilance, and minimal equipment.

For beans, peas, corn, lettuce, and ornamentals, it is simply a matter of watchful patience. Let the plant do the work for you by letting the fruit remain on the plant until the pod has dried (in the case of beans and peas) or until the dried seeds are almost ready to fall off or blow away. Particularly for beans and peas, we stress that the perfect time to harvest the seeds is when you can hold your hand under the pods and let the seed fall into it. Lighter seed heads that depend on the wind to distribute them require only a little more patience. For example, in the case of lettuce or salsify, you must be sure to check the plants daily (twice a day is a good idea) and pluck the seeds along with the white fuzz before it blows away.

For melons the process is easier but a whole lot messier! The seeds extract sugar from the fruit while still imbedded inside. Your seeds will be most viable if, after harvesting very ripe fruit, you let it sit until it begins to soften on the outside. Open up the fruit and scoop out the seeds, rinse them off and spread them on a paper towel until dry.

Cucumber and tomatoes are the most complicated because they must go through a fermentation process before you can store them. Tomatoes can be harvested as they ripen, but cucumbers should be left on the vine until they are very over ripe. The number of family and friends you are saving seeds for will determine how many seeds you will be working with. Seeds from a few fruit can go very far.

Begin by scooping the seeds encased in their gel sacs (the membrane that surrounds the seeds) into a glass jar. Here at the Heirloom Seed Project, the preferred scooping instrument is our fingers! After you scooped the seeds from the tomatoes, put a little water in the jar, stir, label the jar with the name and the date you seeded the fruit and place the jar in a cool, dry place. You can cover it lightly with a paper towel and secure with a rubber band as the fermenting process does get smelly! Do not cover tightly with a lid and do not fill the jars more than ¾ full to allow for escaping gas. After about three days of fermenting, (this varies with the temperature of the air), a sludge will form on top of the mixture. This consists of mold, useless seeds, and bits of pulp. Good (viable) seeds sink to the bottom of the jar and useless seeds float to the top. You can stir the mixture each day to help release any good seeds caught in the sludge. The purpose of fermenting the seeds is to destroy mold and fungi spores which could harm the seed and decrease germination rates. Allowing the seeds to ferment too long encourages the protective gel sac around each seed to break down, causing the seeds to sprout.

Once the sludge layer has formed, it is usually safe to wash the seeds. Scoop off the worst of the sludge and start draining off the rest of the liquid. As the liquid is pouring off, you're getting rid of the useless seeds which have floated to the top during fermentation. When you see that you're reaching the seeds at the bottom of the jar, stop pouring and fill the jar with clean, cold water. Allow the seeds to settle again, and pour off the liquid. Repeat until the seeds are washed and clean and the water is clean.

The next step in the saving of seed is crucial:

Once your seeds have been harvested and processed (fermented or shelled), they should be allowed to open air dry. Place the seeds on a paper towel on a flat dish or pan (we use plant flats) and place them out of direct light in a climate-controlled place where they will have little chance of being disturbed by curious children, cats or (worst yet) mice. Be sure to label the paper towels. Gently stir them around on the paper towel each day to prevent them from sticking together.

Continued on page 207 | At Landis Valley seeds are raised in many venues—in dedicated growing fields and in show gardens, mostly tended by volunteers. Some common vegetables produce amazing flowers like the yellow turnip blooms and the convoluted beet flowers.

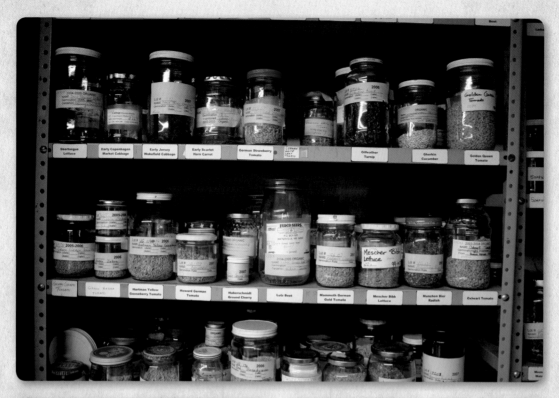

A year's harvest of seeds is stored in tightly sealed glass jars. A drape is drawn to keep light from them when they are awaiting packing and not posing for photographs.

Most tomato seeds look alike. Careful labeling and handling are essential.

Seed packing is a hand process.

A variation of this process is followed by tomato grower *extraordinaire* Amy Goldman, author of *The Heirloom Tomato*, who uses paper plates, carefully labeled directly as a marker. At harvest time, most flat surfaces of her Hudson Valley, New York, home are covered with marked paper plates of seeds, cradling her precious seed harvest.

Within a few days the seeds should be dry enough to store for the winter. It is best to store seeds in an airtight container and in a cool, dry and light-free space, such as your refrigerator. Word of caution…if you store your seeds in the refrigerator or freezer, let them warm to room temperature before you open the jar. It is best not to mix seeds from different years. Sometimes genetic crossings don't show up right away, so you want to have a way of tracing and confining a problem should one occur.

At any given time the Heirloom Seed Project is researching, trailing, or preserving about 200 different varieties of vegetables, herbs, and ornamentals and, not surprisingly, the most popular seeds are tomatoes and beans. The Heirloom Seed Project's attention to tomatoes long precedes the contemporary craze, which is an early twenty-first-century phenomenon. *New York Magazine* (September 6, 2004) noted that the "Heirloom mania has so gripped the collective culinary consciousness, [The Tasting Room's Colin Alevra] says, 'it would be almost daring now to serve just a beefsteak'—even the good ones that come along in August."

If anything, the trend or craze has intensified. A visit to any upscale restaurant will prove the point; however, it is rare for all individual varieties to be named. Salads employing tomatoes of varied shades remain popular and, in the age of the locavore, the name of the grower and location are often given with a solemnity formerly only accorded to very expensive bottles of wine.

Dry seeds await a final sorting and packing in the Seed House.

Rutgers University's agricultural department conducts ongoing experimentation to identify the best heirlooms to grow in New Jersey. The ultimate compliment to the glorification of the heirloom tomato is the creation of counterfeit heirlooms. Procacci Brothers of Philadelphia, the largest supplier of table tomatoes in America, is now promoting the UglyRipe, a deeply fissured tomato that looks like an heirloom and has a distinctive taste—and ships well. The company had to challenge Florida agricultural standards for commercial tomato production that called for the tomato of commerce to be properly symmetrical with a smooth skin.

The Heirloom Seed Project collects, grows, and researches heirloom tomatoes, especially potato-leaf strains, often referred to as "German type" tomatoes. These varieties are unique because their leaves are shaped like potato leaves. The fruits of these tomatoes tend to be lobed, indicating older strains. [They] are indeterminate types, which continue to set blossoms and fruit until frost. They produce long vines. Determinate varieties are compact in growth, and their fruits ripen over a short period of time.

The HSP grows and regularly offers eleven pink/red tomatoes, five orange/yellow ones, and two greens. The reds are Amish paste, Belgian beauty, black Brandywine, German strawberry, Howard German, oxheart, pepper, pink Brandywine, red Brandywine, Reigart, and riesentraube ("giant grape"). The orange/yellows are golden queen, Hartman yellow gooseberry, mammoth German gold, pink grapefruit (skin yellow, flesh pink), and the yellow Brandywine. The greens are Aunt Ruby's green and green zebra. All predate 1900. Interestingly, tomatoes were one of the last of the usual vegetables to be regularly grown by the Dutch. The fruit itself is a native of the Andes Mountains of South America and was introduced into Europe by the Spanish in the early sixteenth century. It was quickly adopted into the cuisine of not only Spain but also southern Italy. As a foodstuff it slowly spread north. Nineteenth-century immigrants from Germany and Russia, like Grandpa Ott, were bringing tomato heirlooms with them. Since the traditional Pennsylvania Dutch are those who arrived in America before 1800, they did not bring ancestral tomatoes with them. As in general American society, the tomato was not commonly cultivated until the late nineteenth century.

The most popular of the tomato varieties the Heirloom Seed Project grows is the Red Brandywine, which to aficionados is the quintessential heirloom variety. Originating in Chester County, its "… flesh is juicy with terrific tomato taste." Like many of today's heirlooms, the Brandywine was first introduced by a commercial seed house. The first to offer it was probably

Seed packages await shipment.

William Henry Maule of Philadelphia in 1869.

Of the tomatoes the Heirloom Seed Project grows, the authors' personal favorites are:

- **AMISH PASTE TOMATO** (pre-1900). Its heart shape makes this a distinctive addition to any vegetable garden. Like our Howard German tomato, Amish paste is an excellent sauce tomato, great in salsas or salads, and tasty all by itself! Best to stake plants.

- **GERMAN STRAWBERRY TOMATO** (pre-1900) Touted as the "Ultimate Sandwich Tomato," this fruit looks like a gigantic strawberry. These uniform fruits average 10 inches in circumference and contain little juice and firm meat. Excellent flavor.

- **HARTMAN YELLOW GOOSEBERRY TOMATO** (pre-1900) This cherry tomato variety is a vigorous producer of 1″ size fruit. It definitely beats out its modern day hybrid relatives in taste with its mildly acidic (or tart) flavor. Imagine what an interesting tomato salad these would make combined with our Riesentraube tomatoes! Best if staked.

Landis Valley doesn't plant fowl. The jar labeled "chicken" contains inferior seeds, which make fine food for Landis Valley's feathery interpreters. Belgium Beauty tomato (left) and balloon flower seeds are in the trays.

(These descriptions and all similar seed descriptions in this chapter are from Landis Valley Heirloom Seed Project materials.)

A new wrinkle in growing heirloom tomatoes is using grafted plants, which is helpful in areas where fusarium wilt or verticillium wilt are problems. As in all grafting, a scion the upper portion of a plant is grafted onto a superior disease resistant rootstock. Unlike fruit tree grafting, this is not a do-it-yourself project, as described by Carol Michel in *Pennsylvania Gardener*:

> ... what is needed for a successful tomato graft is to have a scion and rootstock that are the same diameter. Once the plants are joined together, and held together using a variety of techniques, they are placed in a healing chamber. The healing chamber is sterile, low-light, high-humidity, temperature-controlled environment that helps to keep the scion alive until the graft with the rootstock takes hold and the scion can begin to receive water through the rootstock.

When you plant your grafted heirlooms, you always have to leave the graft about an inch above ground. Otherwise treat your grafted plants like your others, but expect your grafted plants to be bigger with more extensive root systems. W. Atlee Burpee is a major supplier of grafted plants. Among their best sellers is the grafted red Brandywine. The number of books devoted to heirloom tomatoes is impressive. Those which we think are best are noted in the bibliography.

Botanically distantly related to the tomato is the husk tomato or ground cherry (*Physalis pubescens*), a favorite pie fruit among the Pennsylvania Dutch. A number of the *Physalis* family, the fruit is characteristically covered by husk that, even when dry, protects the fruit. As a foodstuff its close cousin is the much larger tomatillo, (*Physalis philadelphica*) or husk tomato, especially used in Hispanic cuisine. A showy relation is the Japanese lantern (*Physalis alkengi*) which is prized for its persistent ornamental orange husks and was grown in many Dutch gardens. Ground cherries are easily grown from seed directly sown into warm soil after frost danger is past. Seed can be persistent and the plant often self-sows. The technique for saving the tiny seeds from these fruits is unique but easy, according to the HSP:

> Clean the papery husks off of the mature, yellowed fruit and toss them in a blender. Add enough water to cover the fruit and puree them. Be sure to put the top on your blender before turning it on or you will have a real mess! The seeds are small enough that the blades of the blender will not destroy them. Once you have created a fine pulp, pour into a pitcher and stir vigorously to separate the seeds from the pulp. Like tomatoes and cucumbers, the good seeds will sink to the bottom and the empty seeds and pulp will float to the top. Now it is a matter of pouring off the material that is floating on the top. Continue to add water until the pulpy material is minimal. Pour mixture through a paper towel to filter the seeds. Spread seeds on a clean paper towel and dry.

The HSP offers one variety:

- **HUBERSCHMIDT: GROUND CHERRY** (pre-1800) *Member of the Physalis family.* Grown historically by Pa. Germans and still today in many gardens, our ground cherry has been a source for pies, jellies and salsas. Some eat this fruit directly out of the garden. But if this is your partiality, be sure to choose only the mature yellow fruit. The fruit has a distinctive tart, tomato flavor with a sweet after-taste. Most will agree, "You'll either love it or hate it!"

Tomato seeds get special processing: fermenting them removes the gel sac around the seeds and kills various molds. Any wide-mouth jar will do. The jars are sealed with paper towels held in place with rubber bands. These porous covers also make great labels. After about three days, kept away from direct sunlight, the good seeds sink to the bottom. Discard seeds and other impurities form a sludge that floats to the surface. This process is also used with cucumber seeds.

One author relishes eating the fruit out of hand, the other knows people who grow it, but neither he nor his family ever had anything to do with the ground cherry.

The HSP offers neither peppers nor eggplants. Traditionally they were not grown by the Dutch but by the post-World War II years, stuffed green peppers became common cuisine and green bell peppers were grown. At the Herb and Garden Faire the HSP now offers a wide range of pepper plants, reflecting more contemporary Dutch tastes. Common adoption of eggplant is much later and eggplant dishes remain uncommon in Dutch cuisine.

Less showy and glamorous than the tomato is the bean, another heirloom vegetable assuming star status—especially in dried form. On chic menus the beans are often mentioned by varietal names. Dried beans are always available and remain consistent. The beans may look especially beautiful and distinctive in the state when they are inedible. Fresh beans, which have a briefer season, are seldom identified by name although many of these are distinctive in taste and attractive to the eye.

The HSP offers beans divided into four categories: bush beans, lima beans, pole beans, and wax beans. Many have colorful names. Bush beans are compact and do not need staking.

The ten bush beans include Aunt Ina's glass, kerley, Jacob's cattle bean, Lizzie Baer, and mull kidney. Five especially interesting ones are:

- **FISHER BEAN** (pre-1850). This bush bean has been grown by a Lancaster County, Pa., farm family for many years. According to foodways expert and writer, William Woys Weaver, the Fisher Bean is the same as the old Pennsylvania Dutch Oibuhne "Egg bean" or Eenbuhne "All in one bean." Weaver states that the bean is mentioned in 1820 in the Rhineland, and he has traced its origin to the Iroquois in eastern North America. Will thinks it was known to the Lenni-Lenape Indians. The Fisher bean can be used as a dry or snap bean, but its small size, round shape, and circle around the eye, make it an attractive dry bean. Good yields and, when cooked, it is quite tasty.

- **GRANDMA STOBER'S CHOW CHOW BEAN (PRE-1850) FROM LANCASTER COUNTY, PA.** This is the bean used in the popular Pa. Dutch chow chow relish dishes. The bean is white with a red eye and holds its shape when cooked. It is extremely prolific after maturing in 90 days. A close relative of this bean is the Soldier Bean from New England.

- **HUTTERITE SOUP BEAN** (pre-1750) The Hutterite soup bean came to this country from a communal sect of German Anabaptists. It is a bush bean and, traditionally, the pods are allowed to dry on the vine before harvesting. The dried beans are then used in soup. This productive bean matures early, 75–85 days. The seed is round, buff-yellow with a greenish hue.

- **MRS. NEIDIGH'S SIX WEEK BEAN** (pre-1850) This snap bush bean has been grown by a Lancaster County, Pa., family for many years. It has an excellent flavor but does require stringing before cooking. This heavy producer has a white seed. As with most beans, it can be dried for soups.

- **SACRAMENT BEAN** (pre-1900) Migrating from Germany, this dry bush bean can be used in soups, baking and salads. The bean is medium sized. It is interesting to observe that most of the white seeds with maroon

markings around the hilum resemble a monstrance (a vessel in which the consecrated Host is exposed for the veneration of the faithful). At any rate, it holds its colors and shape nicely when cooked in addition to having a good bean flavor. It matures in 80 days.

Both religion and superstition are strong undercurrents in Pennsylvania German gardening, as pointed out in chapter II, and so too, religious imagery occasionally appears in the naming of seed varieties.

The lima bean, unlike most other common beans, is not classified as *Phaseolus vulgaris*, but as *Phaseolus lunatus* and, accordingly, it will not cross with other beans, but is very friendly with other limas. Consequently, if you want to save your own seeds, be sure to isolate the different varieties that, unlike the limas of the mass vegetable trade, can vary in color as well as taste. The HSP offers four varieties—the least well documented is Verna Shirk lima bean (age unknown). Donated to the HSP by a local family, the baby lima bean is maroon with pink marbling. The HSP notes, "The family who donated this bush bean used the beans for chow-chow and soup."

- **ALMA'S LIMAS** (pre-1900) This pretty little bean has been grown by a local family for many years. The original beans were thought to have been brought to Lancaster County, Pa., from Germany by the family's great-great grandfather. Although it is considered to be a pole bean, it is not a vigorous climber. A two-foot trellis would be high enough to support the vine. The seed is black-burgundy in color, but occasionally a white bean seed is produced. High yield.

- **PA GERMAN RED LIMAS** (pre-1900) These heirloom pole beans have been grown in Lancaster County, Pa., for their flavor. The Pa. German red limas are somewhat similar in growth habit and appearance to Alma's limas and there is some speculation that they are the same bean. However, the Pa. German red limas do not produce the occasional white bean seed. We would be interested in hearing what results other people have in growing these beans. As a cooked vegetable, these beans, as well as Alma's, have a sweet, nutty flavor.

Lima beans still in their pods and those shelled, waiting to be sorted.

The HSP best-selling bean of all is:

- **DR. MARTIN'S POLE LIMAS** (pre-1900) Dr. Martin's can be quite vigorous in their growth habit with vines up to 12 feet in length, but they seem to prefer climbing a trellis to the more traditional teepee poles. The pods are usually 5 inches in length and contain 3 to 4 large beans. There are a number of lima bean devotees at the Heirloom Seed Project who would proclaim these limas to have the best flavor in the whole world. Best planted around the beginning of June. Matures in 90-100 days.

Pole beans are climbers and many are very vigorous. The traditional manner is to grow them on teepees made of saplings. Today we often use poles or bamboo and keep our rows six feet apart. Because pole beans easily cross, if you want to save seeds, never grow more than one variety per teepee. To use the beans dry, or for seed, leave them on the vine for at least six weeks to thoroughly ripen and dry. Pole beans mature from the bottom up, and not at one time, so keep picking them as they dry.

The HSP offers five varieties – all are interesting and one, the scarlet runner bean, is one of the group's oldest seeds of any variety.

- **SCARLET RUNNER BEAN** (pre-1750) This heirloom bean has a dual purpose to serve in its life cycle. Many people grow this bean solely for the pretty red blossoms that grow on the long vines. Others take advantage of the culinary uses of the dried bean. In the dried stage, the large seed is a strikingly beautiful black bean with purple markings. Can be grown anywhere it has support and can climb, even up corn stalks! Children love to grow this one. Matures in 65-90 days.

Two nineteenth-century beans are:

- **AMISH GNUTTLE BEAN** (pre-1850) Dating to the 1840s, this pole bean is similar in appearance to the Gnuttle cutshort bean. A wonderful description of the Amish gnuttle bean follows: a square-ended, short, roundish, maroon-flecked, tannish-grey seed. It truly holds up to its description and adds interest, as well as taste, to the soup pot. When cooked alone, the texture is soft and creamy. An added bonus is its propensity toward high yields after maturing in 90 days.

- **WREN'S EGG POLE BEAN** (pre-1825) This bean is also known as the speckled cranberry bean. It is an old variety that has been grown in kitchen gardens for many years. It should be noted that pole beans are prolific and everbearing up to the first frost. This bean is no exception. Easy to shell like peas, the beans are cooked fresh or can be frozen for later use. The pods are wide, thick and about 5" long. The bean is tan with maroon speckles and streaks when dried and it really does resemble a wren's egg.

The most interesting story related to any bean (or any other vegetable) in the HSP, or any, collection is the tale of the Mostoller wild goose. In 1865 a flock of migrating Canada geese landed on the millpond of sawyer Joseph Mostoller in

Somerset County, Pennsylvania. His sons shot several of the fowl and took them home for food. When mother Mosteller prepared to cook them she found whole beans in the crop of one or more of the geese [the story varies]. Curious, she saved the beans and planted them the next spring. Amazed by the plants, she and her daughters and granddaughters shared the resulting beans with others. Modern genetic testing has traced the bean to one still raised by Indians in the northern reaches of Canada. Offered in the HSP first mimeographed seed list in 1986:

- **MOSTOLLER WILD GOOSE** (Dry/Pole): Matures in 55 days; when young is a good snap bean, otherwise use green or dry shell; 90-100 days full maturity. This is a white bean with tan-brown eye and is very productive. Seed was from the crop of a goose shot in Penna. Heirloom grown by Mosteller's et al. for 120 years.

Offered as a climbing bean, but really a Cowpea, is the pretzel bean, *Vigna unguiculata*, a convoluted variant of a bean whose close, but straight, cousin is often called the "yard long bean." Advice from the HSP suggests that you: "Plant in blocks of 6-9 plants, stake with 6' poles and you will get a beautiful tall plant with lavender flowers and curly pods at the top!- much like a pretzel. Can be cooked as you would string beans when harvested young." The dried beans are white with the characteristic brown-black mark of the cowpea, most beloved in Southern cooking.

The HSP offers only one wax bean:

- **BESTE VON ALLEM WAX BEAN** (pre-1900) We originally acquired this seed through Seed Savers Exchange. The pods are long and yellow and the seeds are white with a black eye. These beans make a nice contrast when mixed and cooked with green beans. In fact, many Pennsylvania Germans use this bean in traditional bean salads [including Chow Chow]. It takes 60 to 75 days for this bush bean to mature. Production slows down in extremely hot weather.

The bean's fellow legume, the pea, is a cool weather crop, which must be planted early so that it can mature before temperatures soar. Peas are a favored crop in the kitchen garden and a spring delicacy. The Dutch traditionally grew two types of peas—hull peas, those eaten especially for the pea, and edible pod peas, where the entire pod was eaten. Most favored were varieties that produced plump edible pods. These later were celebrated as "lazy wife peas" —because they didn't need hulling. The Dutch didn't eat pea tendrils, an end of the twenty-first century delicacy borrowed from Asian cooking.

Traditionally peas were grown on trellises, or "pea sticks," made of branches pruned from apple trees. In mid-March, sow the seed about 1 inch deep and allow 1–2 inches between seeds in rows 24–36 inches apart. Trellis when the seedlings appear, being careful not to damage the root system. To increase support for the vines and provide more planting space, plant double rows of like variety about 6 inches apart, and trellis between the rows. Rotate pea crops year to year.

The HSP offers four peas, one hull and three "lazy wife."

- **GRANDMA HERSHEY'S SUGAR PEAS** (pre-1900) This pea is from the Isaac Hershey family, the developer of Lancaster Sure Crop corn. Grow this pea on support. The Hershey family told us that they usually allow the seed to develop in the pod rather than eat the pea in the flat pod stage. It is apparently still tender when the seeds are slightly further along in development. This variety yields well. Not quite as early as the Risser early sugar pea.

- **PRUSSIAN BLUE PEA** (1825) A hull pea originally from Germany, this low growing variety (still needs trellising) produces pretty blue-green smooth seeds, about 5–6 per pod. The pods have a blue cast to them. This variety yields well in 75–95 days.

- **RISSER EARLY SUGAR PEA** (pre-1850) Lancaster County heirloom grown by several generations of the Risser family. Edible-podded, a nice producer; good flavor; tall vines.

- **RISSER SICKLE PEA** (pre-1800) This variety is from the same family as the Risser early sugar pea. Risser sickle pea is edible podded; and is a heavy producer with sickle-shaped pods. The seed is slightly squared in shape. Grow on trellises.

Spring was also the time for lettuce, which was used differently by the Pennsylvania Dutch than it is today. Lettuce was used primarily in wilted salads, as were the often wild-collected dandelion greens. Typically a warm bacon or cream-based dressing was used. The Dutch, along with most farm families of whatever nationality, traditionally do not favor raw foods.

The three most common kinds of lettuce we cultivate are head, leaf, and cos (Romaine). Annual lettuce will produce seed if it is allowed to "bolt"—send up a flower stalk. It is always best to choose the latest-bolting plants. Lettuce varieties will cross and cultivated lettuce will cross with wildings. To keep your seeds pure, the HSP notes it is best practice "... to cover the plants with a cage or floating row cover" right before they blossom. Remove the cover when the seeds start to set:

Lettuce seed ripens at varying rates, but is usually ready 10-24 days after flowering. Check lettuce each day during the flower stage. You can harvest individual dry blossoms, which is time consuming , or gently bend the seed stalk over and into a large paper bag, and tap the flower head against the bag sides to knock the seeds into the bag. Continue to do this during the blooming period.

Hyacinth beans and deertongue lettuce seeds (back).

The HSP's three lettuces are:

- **BLACK SEEDED SIMPSON LETTUCE** (1850) An early leaf lettuce, with a mild, sweet flavor. Black seeded Simpson has been a favorite for many years. Grow in spring and fall; fairly hot-weather tolerant, curled leaves.

- **DEERTONGUE LETTUCE** (1740) This is an old lettuce variety which is a favorite among Pa. Germans and others. Fairly slow to bolt, this lettuce forms an upright, loose head with light green triangular shaped leaves, thought to resemble a deer's tongue. The flavor is sweet with a nice crisp texture, especially when young.

- **MESCHER BIBB LETTUCE** (1700s) A very old lettuce, this Bibb type lettuce produces small heads of wavy green leaves, tinted with red. It has an excellent flavor. Produces well in cold weather. Very limited amount.

The other leafy vegetables the HSP grows are spinach and kale, which, like lettuce, are cool weather crops. **SPINACH** (*Spinacia oleracea*) is a good fall crop and can be planted up until early winter when the ground freezes. Protect with mulch, as a late planting will give you an early spring crop. In raising spinach for seed there are several caveats says the HSP:

As the day lengthens, spinach bolts to seed. Spinach plants produce either male or female flowers. To assure good pollination and maintain genetic diversity, it is necessary to have the proper ratio of male and female flowers. This can be accomplished by planting close in wide seed beds. Don't crowd spinach, as this contributes to early bolting. There are varieties of spinach which are bred to be tolerant to long days or cold weather.

The HSP's only variety:

- **BROAD-LEAVED PRICKLY SPINACH** This old variety of spinach has large, thick, deep green leaves. It is a longstanding variety and can be sown in spring or fall; it is very hardy. The seed is prickly.

- **KALE** (Brassica oleracea) is a very hardy biennial, that tends to resist both cold and heat. Since kale toughens with age, it is best to harvest the leaves young.

If you are going to let this biennial go to seed the second year, harvest the first year's green sparingly. Remember that kale is a member of the Brassica family and will cross with cabbage, cauliflower, broccoli and brussels sprouts.

The HSP grows only one of this suddenly very popular vegetable, which has become a darling of the healthy and fashionable eating crowd.

- **RUSSIAN KALE (RAGGED JACK OR RUGGED JACK KALE)** (pre-1885) A mildly acidic, but bold flavor, this ancient variety is very hardy. A delicate, oak-leaved appearance, this variety is not only tasty, but also a wonderful visual addition to your garden.

COLLARDS or collard greens, another group of cultivars of *Brassica oleracea*, which has become popular was essentially unknown to the Dutch.

In the world of the upscale restaurant it is impossible to escape from the roasted beet and an assortment of multicolored carrots. Both beets and carrots were prized among the Pennsylvania Germans for their taste, color, and keeping ability. Along with turnips, leeks, and black salsify, they are the HSP's root crops.

BEETS (*Beta vulgaris*) are a biennial, which is a problem for seed savers. Because the root is produced the first year, and the flowers and seeds the second, the beetroot must be overwintered—either by heavily mulching your stock in the ground or by carefully digging the beets in the fall, storing them in a root cellar over the winter, and then replanting them in the spring. Heirloom beets are different than modern hybrids because growers favored large size above flavor nuance. Beets also were prized for their rich red color. Red beet eggs, pickled with cider vinegar, spices, and sugar, are a Pennsylvania German mainstay. Perfect hard-boiled eggs mixed with pickled beets turn a bright red. Beets with some white striation were appreciated for their novelty. Yellow beets were almost unheard of. The rainbow salads of roasted beets served with goat cheese and toasted nuts was unknown. Beet greens were also often cooked as a vegetable. The HSP offers two varieties of beets:

- **DEACON DAN BEET** (pre-1850) A very large beet. This variety gets its name from the accounts that it dates back to the gardens to Deacon Dan Burkholder. This is a long season beet that keeps well in cold storage and will retain its sweet, tender qualities as it increases in size. When raw, Deacon Dan is striated red and white, turns to a light gold color when heated and to pure deep red when cooled. An extremely tasty beet that is delicious served with butter or vinegar.

- **LUTZ BEET** (pre-1828) The Lutz beet is also known as the "New Century Beet." Some HSP gardeners feel that its flavor surpasses the Deacon Dan Beet for sweetness. It is another tasty beet that keeps well through the winter months, but can also be eaten raw when harvested young. This beet also starts out with red and white striations. Try it for yourself and note the color changes as it cooks. Matures in 60–80 days.

The **CARROT** (*Daucus carota*) is a member of the *Umbelliferae* family and a close relative of Queen Anne's lace—a beautiful wildflower also referred to as the wild carrot. In fact, it is believed that all modern carrots are descended from Queen Anne's lace. Accordingly, all carrots will crossbreed with Queen Anne's lace, which is found everywhere. For the seed saver, this is a problem. If you can't guarantee that you are at least a half-mile from the nearest Queen Anne's lace plant, you must hand-pollinate and cage your carrots—among the most promiscuous of vegetables! Carrots occur naturally in white (the color of Queen Anne's lace roots), blues, and oranges. Blues were especially favored in Eastern Europe. Germans favored orange ones and especially grew them in raised-bed gardens where soil could be sifted to be stone free. The favored heirloom most commonly offered is:

- **EARLY SCARLET HORN CARROT** (pre-1710) Short and stubby, this variety yields early in the growing season. A great carrot that keeps its fresh tasty flavor after it's frozen or cooked.

The **TURNIP**, *Brassica rapa*, like most of its *brassica* relatives, likes cool weather and the roots can overwinter in the ground. This is handy since, as a biennial, it blooms the second year. Turnips are traditionally thinned once the leaves are large enough to use as greens: they are a German favorite cooked with a smoked ham hock. The HSP's is:

- **GILFEATHER TURNIP** (pre-1900) A Vermont variety, this turnip has a delicious sweet taste. The top-shaped, creamy white root is knobby. It is excellent eaten raw! Good cooked too! It is believed to be from Germany originally.

The HSP does not offer any **RUTEBAGA** (*Brassica Napobrassica*), which was known but less commonly grown.

Curiously, the Heirloom Seed Project hasn't any of the familiar root **RADISHES** (*Raphanus sativus*) or *reddich*—a strange omission since they are a common vegetable in the Pennsylvania German diet. Perhaps they are too common, too easily grown, and two bountiful in their seed production, and the seeds are readily available everywhere. The Dutch grew mostly springtime radishes—and popular heirloom varieties include white Icicles, early Scarlet glove, French breakfast, and German giant. Some Dutch also grew the black Spanish, a winter radish well known in Europe where it was best known by its French name, *Gros Noir d'Hiver*. However the HSP does offer seeds for the Munchen bier radish (*Raphanus caudatus*), which is a nineteenth-century German import, via the Far East. Unlike the more familiar radishes, the Munchen bier is grown for its seed pods, which are eaten fresh as a spicy beer accompaniment and were also pickled. Also unlike other radishes, it grows best in hot weather and continues to bear pods over a long period. Because of their shape, the radish is often called the Rats tail podding radish by the English. Of course, all radish varieties will bloom and go to seed, but only the podded varieties are generally eaten.

ONIONS are ubiquitous in Pennsylvania German cuisine, both as fresh green onions in spring or the more familiar round yellow onion, the most commonly grown species of the genus *Allium*. Since most people grow their onions from "sets" or small bulbs, the HSP does not handle onions or garlic, which plays a very small role, if any, in traditional Pennsylvania German cookery. The vegetable allium that they do offer is the leek, a biennial whose seed production is prodigious.

LEEKS (*Allium ampeloprasum v. porrum*) require special cultivation, which in essence bleaches them, notes the HSP:

Seeds should be sown indoors about 8 weeks before last frost date. Transplant seedlings in a trench about 1 foot deep and 6–8 inches wide. Use compost to fill the trench a few inches and place the seedlings about 6 inches apart. Fill the trench to cover the base of the bulb as it matures. A sunny, moist, well-drained section of your garden is the perfect spot for a planting of leeks. Leeks will not cross with other alliums.

The Heirloom Seed Project offers:

- **SWISS GIANT COLOMA LEEK** (pre-1900) This is a good early variety with long blanched cylindrical bulbs. It is a good producer, tasty in salads, soups and other main entrees (especially good sautéed with mushrooms). If left to go to seed, these plants will provide a very decorative addition to your garden with their grand flower heads.

Another common Dutch-related vegetable that is traditionally bleached during the growing process is **CELERY** (*Apium graveolens var. dulce*), almost all of which is a variety called Pascall. Although commonly grown by the Germans, the HSP does not offer any seeds, nor do they for the lesser known Celeriac or Celery Root (*Apium graveolens var. rapaceum*). At Amish weddings, serving creamed celery is a must. A general observation is that if a lot of celery is being grown in the garden of a family with daughters, a wedding is in the offing.

The last of HSP's root vegetables is the **BLACK SALSIFY** (*Scorzonera hispanica*), which the Dutch called *Schwarzwetzel*. It is also available in a white-skinned variety, which is most common in the larger world. It is often called oyster plant, oyster root, or vegetable oyster. The authors believe that you need an active, specialized imagination to make the gustatorial connection.

Salsify is a biennial that requires a long growing period and benefits from cold weather. It can be left in the ground and harvested in the spring. Even if you are not into seed saving you should let some go to flower. The black salsify's flower is yellow, the white-skinned variety is blue. In both cases the flowers are followed by seedheads that look like giant dandelions. A very nontraditional use for the seedhead is to carefully spray it with hairspray and then cut it and use it in autumn displays. Except for skin color, there apparently are no varieties. The HSP simply offers:

- **BLACK SALSIFY** (pre-1800) This seed is from Lancaster County. There are male and female seeds; female seeds are plumper and fewer in number than the thinner male seeds; plant some of each to ensure seed production. The dark green leaves are long and tapered with a groove down the center, and appear to spring right from the ground. In the second year, if allowed to remain in the garden, a seed stalk will shoot up bearing large, daisy-like yellow flowers.

Grown in the same way as salsify are **PARSNIPS** (*Pastinaca sativa*), which the Dutch also used but, again, HSP does not offer any seeds of the limited range of available varieties.

CORN (*Zea mays*), an American native, was grown in the Palatinate before the great eighteenth-century migration, used mostly as animal food. In America it became a regular part of the human diet, first for meal and popcorn. It wasn't until late in the eighteenth century that the Germans began growing sweet corn—originally young tender variants of field corn. In the nineteenth century sweet corn, selected for its special qualities, began being cultivated for table use.

Traditionally corn was planted six to eight seeds in hills and thinned to the three to four healthiest plants. Corn was often interplanted with squash and pole beans. The prickly quality of squash leaves and stems kept some pests at bay and the corn stalks provided support for the beans. You always gave the corn at least a ten-day head start on the beans. The HSP offers:

- **SHAFFER 8-ROW SWEET CORN** (pre-1900) Over 100 years old, this variety came to us from our neighbor county of York, PA. This is a mid-season corn that has a small cob with large grains. A unique feature of Shaffer 8-row is its tendency to produce suckers. Because this corn is apt to wind lodge, it is better to plant in rows and hill around the roots as needed.

- **PENNSYLVANIA DUTCH BUTTER FLAVORED POPCORN** (pre-1885) This is an heirloom variety of corn, grown by the Pa. Dutch, dating back to the 1800s. It matures in about 105 days with usually 4–6 ears of small

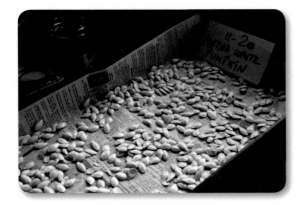

creamy colored kernels per stalk. [The plant is not always prolific.] We have only this year grown enough for seed that we can offer it again to our customers. After harvesting our crop this year, we "sacrificed" an ear so that we could have a taste of this popcorn. True to its name, this popcorn does have a very mild buttery flavor. The popped kernels are snow white and crispy. A great treat.

- **STOWELL'S EVERGREEN CORN** (pre-1848) A sweet, white corn that is a favorite among our customers. It has an extended growing season with plants that produce tender, flavorful kernels on large ears.

The HSP has also offered seneca corn, what most people call Indian corn, a multicolor variety grown mostly for its decorative qualities but that can be made into cornmeal. HSP also has red broom dorn, which is not a corn at all but a *Sorghum* grown for the stiff tassels used to make brushes and brooms. HSP's leading field crop is Lancaster Sure Crop, a very tall grower that has been widely used as a parent plant in the development of modern dent field corn.

The mostly vining, inter-related crops—cucumbers, melons, squash, pumpkins, and gourds—have a long history among the Dutch. Some crops were familiar, at home in Alsace and the Palatinate, to early emigrants. Their seeds had arrived in Europe centuries before the great population exodus.

Cucumbers and pickles are almost synonymous and the Dutch are famous for their many ways of preserving not only cucumbers, but many other fruits and vegetables. The legend of the "Seven Sweets and Seven Sours" holds that no meal was complete without preserved sides or relishes, and it has some basis in fact: along with many farm people, the Germans traditionally did not trust raw vegetables and they employed many ways to preserve them. There were no *crudité* for rural folk.

The HSP offers two cucumber varieties, the earliest of which, the gherkin, is synonymous with a small preserved, often sweet, cucumber.

- **GHERKIN CUCUMBER** (pre-1793) A small pickling cucumber with a light green spiny skin. A vigorous grower, so leave plenty of room in your garden for this vine to spread. A prolific producer, the Gherkin ducumber will give you plenty of fruit to preserve or enjoy fresh.

Dry seneca (Indian) corn kernels removed from their cobs await packing.

- **WHITE CUCUMBER** (pre-1900) This creamy white variety of cucumber is a great addition to your vegetable garden. Sweet and aromatic, the white cucumber is a favorite in our home gardens. If you want to save the seed, just let the cucumber stay on the vine until it is bright orange and the skin and flesh are very soft. This is a variety that we encourage you to try.

CANTALOUPE STYLE MELONS (*Cucumis melo*) grow especially well in the Dutch heartland. Restaurateur and Pennsylvania German cookbook author Betty Groff remembers as a girl being sent down to her father's famed melon patch to bring up a perfect sun-warmed melon to serve to their guest, the legendary James Beard. The two *Cucumis melo* the HSP offers are both green-fleshed.

- **JENNY LIND MELON** (pre-1850) This old fashioned melon is sweet and aromatic. The green-fleshed melons are 1–2 pounds in weight and have a slightly flattened appearance. This variety is worth growing for the wonderful flavor.

- **ROCKY FORD** (1881) This melon, also called "Eden gem," is probably one of the oldest green-fleshed muskmelons. Some list this by another name, "nutmeg," but it is thought that the rocky ford is a cultivar of nutmeg. This melon has a delicious sweet flavor and a spicy aroma. Rocky ford is early and produces heavy yields.

Two other melons, belonging to *Citrullus lanatus*, are also among the HSP offerings. The most interesting is the citron melon whose seed line dates to 1700.

Our original source for this seed is the Dot and Dick Gerz family in Lancaster, Pa.; looks like a round baby watermelon. Flesh is firm and creamy colored to greenish-white. On its own it has a very neutral taste, probably best to call it tasteless, but this is the melon used to make candied citron. When the flesh is boiled in sugar syrup, it's used in cakes, cookies, and other pastries.

Here the melon is being used as a substitute for the candied rind of the citron (*Citrusmedica*), a Mediterranean lemon-like fruit.

Our other *lanatas* is:

- **MOON AND STARS WATERMELON** (1910) This is a nice melon! Considered an old Amish heirloom variety, it has large yellow moons and small yellow stars on a smooth, dark green, slightly ridged rind. Fruits vary in size for us, and some are more vividly marked than others. The leaves are sprinkled with yellow stars. The seed is dark brown, marked with tan. The flesh of this watermelon is pink-red, and is wonderfully sweet. Allow plenty of space for these big vines. Matures in 95–105 days.

Interestingly, this variety is also popular in the Deep South, especially in Alabama and Mississippi. Watermelons were popular in the Pennsylvania Dutch Country and were often served at church picnics.

SQUASH generally refers to four species of the genus *Cucurbita*, which in America are loosely subdivided into "summer" and "winter" squash, depending on whether they are harvested immature (summer) or mature (winter). Botanically speaking,

pumpkins are squash. While the Dutch commonly grew pumpkins and a variety of other winter squash—including acorn, butternut, and Hubbard— as well as several summer ones—most notably the yellow crookneck and the pattypan—only pattypan seeds are offered by the HSP. In today's foodie culture, where immature vegetables are in fashion, the prolific pattypan provides many small opportunities.

The Pennsylvania Dutch were not very fond of pumpkin vines because of their wide-ranging habits. Some even equated the plants with the devil—this was no doubt reinforced by a borrowing from the Anglo world the practice of carving pumpkins into Jack-o'-Lanterns. Pumpkins were raised for pies and animal feed as well. Among the orange varieties grown were the small Long Island Cheese (8–15 lbs) and the larger Happy Jack (15–40 lbs). The Heirloom Seed Project offers a pumpkin that was more commonly grown before the Halloween ornament became popular in Dutch culture, the Fortuna White (*Cucurbita pepo var. papol*), a pear shaped white-skinned pumpkin with yellow flesh that is especially good for pies.

GOURDS (*Lagenaria siceraria*) are a close relative of the squash and the immature fruits of many varieties are edible, however, most gourds are raised for their shells, which have been used since biblical times. Vigorous growers, they do best on a strong bean teepee or along a fence. In saving seeds you want the fruit to mature like a melon or squash; otherwise, dry them. As the HSP notes:

Drying your own gourds is easy but requires a lot of space. Before the first frost, harvest your crop and wipe off soil and moisture. Place your gourds in a dry, cool place where they will get good air circulation and can be spread out. Turn the gourds every few days to help promote even drying and minimize decay, but be prepared to lose a few to rot. Mold may appear on the hardened shells and can be scraped off with a knife. After 2–4 months, the seeds inside will rattle and you will know that your gourds are ready to be used. Use a fine steel wool to clean and polish the shells and decorate. While the Dutch grew ornamental gourds, mostly they grew useful ones. The HSP gourds are functional:

· **BIRDHOUSE GOURD SEED** (pre-1850) This gourd is rounded (almost squat) with a short-to-medium length neck. Perfect for hanging from a tree limb in your yard. Simply drill a hole in the side … With a smaller drill bit, add a few holes in the bottom for drainage, a hole in the top for stringing a leather strap through and a hole below the entrance. The latter hole is to create a roosting spot using a small stick or branch.

· **DIPPER GOURD SEED** (pre-1850) A small round body with a long neck that is perfect for using as a dipper for watering the plants in your garden. Even if the necks are not straight, these gourds can add interest in your gardens. We have a few dipper gourds, whose handles are not straight, hanging from the bean teepees in our 19th century raised bed garden. Every year we welcome a family of wrens into our gardens. It's fun to watch the parents raise their young and listen to their chatter.

· **LARGE BOTTLE GOURD SEED** (pre-1850) Just like the name, these gourds are shaped like a bottle with a rounded lower section, a narrow neck and a slightly elongated upper section. If you stand these gourds upright while they are growing, you will have flat-bottomed gourds that will sit level. After they have dried, you can cut off the tops and hinge both pieces with leather straps and use for storage, or throw away the tops and use as a bowl. Bottle gourds can also be used for birdhouses.

Another functional gourd (that HSP doesn't offer), which is interesting and was often grown is the luffa gourd (*Luffa actangula*), whose cultivation is more complex because of its long growth period. The interior of mature fruits are used as sponges.

The last vegetable to be mentioned is one of the most important crops for the Pennsylvania Germans: **CABBAGE** (*Brassica oleracea var capitata*). Along with the potato (which is commonly grown from seed potatoes, rather than potato seed), cabbage was found in most meals, especially in the winter and early spring. Cabbage not only has good keeping quality in itself, but it can be fermented into sauerkraut. Author William Woys Weaver called his book about the Pennsylvania German foodway *The Sauerkraut Yankees*.

Among the traditional Dutch, cabbage was more likely to be a field crop than a garden one but a specialty, such as Savoy cabbage (*Brassica oleracea convert var sabauda*) might be grown in a garden along with the occasional brussels sprouts (a *gemmifera* variant of *Brassica oleracea*). In the twentieth century the cabbage in general has migrated to the garden. The Heirloom Seed Project offers four varieties:

- **EARLY COPENHAGEN MARKET** Cabbage (pre-1850) An excellent producer with large solid heads. A sweet mild flavor that can be harvested in early summer.

- **EARLY JERSEY WAKEFIELD CABBAGE** (pre-1840s) A pointed headed cabbage, this variety also has an excellent mild flavor. It matures early, but keeps well in the field. Cover lightly during the heat of the day. Matures in 60–75 days.

- **RED DRUMHEAD CABBAGE** (pre-1800) A rounded variety with a flat top, which is where it gets its name. This cabbage will keep well during the winter months. Its flavor is sweet and mild.

- **WINNIGSTADT CABBAGE** (pre-1900) Dated from 1860s, this German variety has firm pointed heads with fluted yellow-green leaves. An intermediate cabbage, the flavor is very good. It will keep well over the winter months. Try an early spring planting and a fall planting.

Two other *Brassica Oleracea* should be mentioned—siblings of head cabbage, they are cauliflower and broccoli. The Pennsylvania Germans knew cauliflower from Germany where pioneering varieties of the northern European annual cauliflower, enfurf and snowball were developed in the eighteenth century. The Dutch creamed and mashed cauliflower and enjoyed it pickled as well. Broccoli was unknown to the Pennsylvania Dutch. It was introduced into America in the late nineteenth century by Italian immigrants and would not become a common vegetable until the 1920s. It has subsequently found its way into Dutch cuisine where it is especially seen in a slaw-type salad where diced florets, shredded carrots, raisins, and minced bacon are served in a sweetened mayonnaise-based dressing.

Many of the Dutch also grew, and continue to grow, the **SWEET POTATO** (*ipomoea batatas*), a South or Central American native is usually propagated by stem or root cuttings or by adventitious roots called "slips" that grow from tuberous roots in storage. Seeds are only used for breeding. Accordingly, the HSP does not offer any "sweets," which are a popular fall crop. In early summer many local outlets in Dutch country offer "sweet potato starts." In a blending of German and general American culture, the vegetable is a must for the Thanksgiving table. Interestingly, the sweet potato is in the same family as the common morning glory (*Ipomoeas purpurea*), a popular flower in Dutch country, and "Grandpa Ott's morning glory" was an inspiration for the founding of Seed Savers.

As mentioned earlier, the Pennsylvania Germans did not add a wide range of seasonings to their cooking, but several herbs were popular in addition to horseradish, which is a rhizome, and saffron, which is a bulb—both plant types that the PSH doesn't handle. Seed saving for herbs and ornamentals is similar to saving those of vegetables, except they are all simply dried. As the HSP notes:

> The seeds that can be saved are formed during the flowering period. When the flower is past maturity, a seed head will form where the flower had bloomed. As with most of the vegetable varieties, let the plant do most of the work for you and allow the seed head to dry on the plant. Most seeds from ornamentals and herbs are very small and it is often easier to snip the entire seed head off the plant with a pair of clippers or scissors. Allow the seeds to dry indoors, in a cool dry area out of direct sunlight. Before storing in a glass container, break apart the seed head to free the individual seeds. Store your seeds in a dark, cool and dry place over the winter. Some of your seeds may need to go through a stratification process, which is to allow the seed to freeze for a period of time before planting in your garden.

The hoop house where seedlings for the Herb and Garden Faire are raised.
In winter it also shelters a few tender plants displayed on the property.

The HSP's herbs, in alphabetical order, begin with **AGRIMONY** (*Agrimonia Europatoria*) a pre-1800 selection, which the Pennsylvania Germans call *aderminnich* and which is largely grown today as an ornamental. Its spikes of yellow flowers are attractive and abundant. Sometimes called Church Steeples, it was used as a yellow dyestuff and medicinally for a variety of ailments. Often incorporated into a spring tonic, it was alleged, according to the HSP, to be, "... good for blood and strengthening the liver." Easily started from seeds, this perennial will self-seed.

AMERICAN PENNYROYAL (*Hedeoma pulogioides*), *gruddabalsem* to the Dutch, is a member of the mint family introduced to colonists by Native Americans. Traditionally valued as a medicine and a tea, it is now known to be unsafe to use internally. Its only practical use today is as an insect repellent. An annual, it will self-seed once it becomes established— which is hit or miss. The Heirloom Seed Project had a difficult time establishing American Pennyroyal in the gardens, but eventually made itself quite comfortable in the shady nineteenth-century garden. Sow your seeds both in the fall and spring to ensure a nice bed of this mint plant.

Another discredited medicinal herb that the Dutch treasured as a tea is **COMFREY** (*Symphytum officinale*). An old adage held that for a long healthy life, one should drink comfrey tea every day. Today we know that the practice can damage the liver—like alcohol but without the fun. A tall perennial plant with attractive purple flowers, the leaves continue to be used by gardeners as a soil amendment. While it grows from seeds, most people start it with plants, hence the HSP doesn't offer it.

CULINARY BASIL (*Ocimum basilicum*), *fersonlingshows* to the Dutch, was used occasionally to flavor sauce. The HSP's pre-1800 variety blooms with pink to lavender flowers.

More widely used in food preparation is **BRONZE FENNEL** (*Foeniculum vulgare*), whose leaves and seeds are an ingredient in baked goods and teas, and are used as a flavoring for candy, thanks to its anise-like flavor. An attractive hardy plant, it was used medicinally as a carminative to reduce flatulence. Made into a syrup it was a remedy for colic.

BURNET, also called Salad Burnet (*Sanguisorba minor*), *Nagel Graut* to the Dutch, is a European native, and we are told it was a favorite of English statesman and author Francis Bacon (1561–1626). "As a culinary herb, Burnet will add a mild taste of cucumber to your salads, butters, vinegars and cold drinks. Use the younger leaves as the older leaves may have a bitter taste. The delicate green foliage will give way to spiky pinkish-scarlet blooms that will self seed throughout your garden."

Another traditional favorite is *Kümmel*, known to the English speaker as **CARAWAY** (*Carum carvi*). As the HSP notes:

> With its distinctive licorice taste, Caraway [and especially its seeds] is a great flavoring for rye breads and confectioneries. It is believed to help aerate heavy soils. Used as a natural relief for flatulence, Caraway was found in many historical raised bed gardens for one reason or another. This plant does not like to be transplanted, so scatter seeds where you want the mature herb to grow. A biennial, Caraway should be planted each spring to ensure an annual supply. Harvest the seeds as soon as they darken.

CHIVES (*Allium schoenprasum*) are used to flavor soups and breads traditionally by the Dutch who called them *Schnidderlich*. Moderns use them in dips and salads. The beautiful light lavender flowers are also salad enhancers. Chives are a prolific self-seeder and pop up everywhere. A close relative is **GARLIC CHIVES** (*Allium tuberosum*) or *Schnittloch*, which the Heirloom Seed Project describes engagingly:

Seeds are sprouted in very familiar-looking food containers. "Grapefruit" is a pink tomato variety.

With seedlings moved into individual pots the growing season is in full swing—
from February through April and early May.

A very prolific self-sower, this plant is terrific for its interpretive value in our historic gardens. We let a little grow outside of our gardens so that as visitors stop to chat, they are met with the light scent of garlic as they step on these members of the *Allium* family. The leaves can be used to flavor soups, salads, and other dishes that would benefit from a light garlic flavor. The starry white clusters of flowers in mid- to late summer add beauty to your garden, but beware, if you do not want this plant to spread, collect the seeds from the seed heads before they burst. Garlic Chives like full sun and well drained soil. You can also use Garlic Chives as a pest repellent by planting it along the edges of your garden.

Another *Allium* herb that the Dutch grew, but the HSP does not offer, is the Egyptian or **WALKING ONION** (*Allium proliferum*), which reproduces from small bulblets where a normal onion would have flowers. The plant is grown mainly as a curiosity, today, but the small, intense-flavored below-ground bulb is prized in cooking. (And the bulblets, after the head bends over to touch the ground, provide a continuing supply of scallions.)

The HSP's **CORIANDER** (*Coriandrum sativum*) seed line dates pre-1800. The Dutch called it *Korianver*. While fresh coriander is celebrated today as **CILANTRO**, a common flavoring in Mexican and Indian foods, the Germans grew it for its seeds, which are commonly used in pickles and occasionally in sausage.

DILL (*AnethWhichum graveolens*), uniquely also *Dill* to the Dutch, is widely used in pickles. While most people use the feathery foliage, some like to include the flowerhead/seedhead. An annual, dill often reseeds. It is also grown for the seeds themselves, which are used to flavor bread, pickles, and some soups.

GERMAN CAMOMILE (*Matricaria recutita*) is called *Kamille*. The HSP's seedline dates pre-1850. This low-growing plant has feathery foliage and small daisy-like flowers. A self-seeding annual, its apple-like scent makes it useful in potpourri, but it is even more highly favored for making tea, which many believe calms the nerves. Some people, however, are allergic to German Chamomile, so be cautious. Chamomile is an excellent companion planting for cucumbers and onions in the garden.

HOREHOUND (*Marrubium vulgare*) was known as *Eedann* or *Eedann Tee* to the Dutch. The HSP's pre-1800 strain represents an essentially medicinal herb. Traditionally used to flavor tea and throat lozenges for coughs and throat problems, this herb is a nice addition to any garden. White flowers appear in summer on this bushy, branching plant. Its green/silver foliage appears wooly. The plant can grow up to three feet tall and will spread easily once it is established. Sow seeds or start indoors to transplant after danger of frost has passed. Horehound likes full sun and soil that is well-drained. It can take some dry conditions.

LOVAGE (*Levisticum officianale*) or *Lebschtechel* is a three- to six-foot-tall perennial herb with a celery-like taste and fragrance, and its hollow stems can be used as straws. It is a culinary herb that was once used medicinally as a diuretic. It was found to be dangerous to the kidneys in large doses, however, and should never be used by pregnant women. Seeds should be started indoors in spring and planted outside after the last frost. This tall plant produces many leaves and small pale, yellow flowers all summer long.

MOLE PLANT (*Euphorbia lathyris*) or *Maulwarfgraut* and **MUGWORT** (*Artemesia vulgare*) or *Akli Fraw* are both herbs originally grown for specific purposes and both are extremely toxic. Mole plant was grown around the perimeter of gardens to keep out burrowing critters. A very attractive plant with green and white striped leaves, it grows up to four feet tall. A self-seeder, it travels in your garden. All parts of the plant are toxic. Mugwort is a perennial originally used to flavor beer, hence the name, but now we know it should never be used internally. It's grown today as an ornamental; dried it is used as an insect repellent.

The Heirloom Seed Project's **PARSLEY** (*Petroselinum crispum*) *Peederli* to the Germans is the antique Hamburg Turnip Rooted, which can be traced to the sixteenth century. It is unusual in that it can be used from head to toe. A flat-leaved variety, its long thick, turnip-like root can be stored for winter use.

SUMMER SAVORY (*Satureja hortensis*) or *Bahnegreidel* is an annual herb that is a larger and sweeter plant than the perennial Winter Savory (*Satureja montana*). This herb likes rich, light soil with lots of sunlight and moderate moisture. It resembles thyme in taste and appearance and is just as useful in cooking. Known locally as "bean herb," it can be grown or cooked with beans to add great flavor. The white/pink/lavender blue flowers can be used decoratively in bouquets and wreaths.

The last of the Heirloom Seed Project's herb seeds both have "sweet" in their names, but they have very different qualities. The seedline for both is prior to 1800.

SWEET CICELY (*Myrrhis odarata*) was called *Kernli Graut* or *Siess Wartzel* and can be invasive but, says the HSP:

Do you need a 3' tall, light green fern-like plant for a moist, partially shaded part of your garden? Sweet Cicely may just be the answer. A hardy perennial with a licorice-like flavor and fragrance, Sweet Cicely's white flowers bloom in May and June. The root has been used medicinally and leaves are used in cooking. It needs to go through a freeze/process, called stratification in order to germinate, so spread the seed in the fall.

SWEET MARJORAM (*Majorana hortensis*) or *Maru* or *Warsht Graut* was also used medicinallyCox:

Once used as a medicinal herb that was thought to be helpful for stomach upsets and colic, it is better known now as a culinary herb, especially with green vegetables, poultry, pork and eggs. It's an annual herb whose sweet fragrance is enhanced by the warmth of full sun. It can be started indoors in early spring and transplanted when the garden soil has had a chance to warm.

Five additional herbs that the Dutch commonly grew and used can be propagated by seed, but are most commonly distributed by plant divisions or rooted cuttings. These include sage, thyme, rosemary, rue, and what the Dutch call "teas" and the rest of the populace call mints.

SAGE or **GARDEN SAGE** (*Salvia officinalis*) or *Salwei*, is a woody perennial or sub-shrub with grayish leaves and blue to purplish flowers. The Dutch brewed a tea from it, but they especially used it as a seasoning for fresh pork sausage.

THYME (*Thymus vulgaris*) or *Gwendel*, a small-leaved perennial, was occasionally used as a flavoring agent and for tea making.

ROSEMARY (*Rosmarinus officinalis*) or *Roschmarei* is a shrubby evergreen plant whose aromatic needle-like leaves have a long history of usage, both medicinally and as a flavoring. Herbalists believe it helps to improve memory. The Dutch used it very sparingly in cooking but did steep a tea from it. Marginally hardy in Dutch Country, it was grown mostly as a potted plant. In the Christian tradition, the herb has strong allusions. While resting, the Virgin Mary is supposed to have spread her blue cloak over a white-blossomed shrub and the flowers turned blue. Hence the plant was the "Rose of Mary," Catholic Pennsylvania Germans often placed a rosemary plant in the center of their four square gardens.

RUE (*Ruta graveolens*) is an attractive plant often grown today for its blueish leaves. In small quantities it added a bitter flavor to food—to be counterbalanced with a lot of sweetness. Rarely used in cooking anymore, the Pennsylvania Dutch, who called it *Raude*, also used it for making a bitter tea. It also had some archaic medicinal uses pertaining to menstruation and as an abortifacient.

MINTS (*Mentha*) were most commonly grown outside of a garden setting because of their invasive nature. Most commonly used for teas were Peppermint (*Mentha x piperita*) and Spearmint (*Mentha spicata*), which were also popular in candy making. Also widely used were Lemon Balm (*Melissa officinalis*), Wooly or Apple Mint (*Mentha suaveolens*), and Bergamot Mint, which refers to two mints, *Mentha citrata*, favored for its flavor, and *Monarda didyma*, cherished for its flowers, but also suitable for tea making, and known to the English as Oswego Tea.

Lastly, any good Pennsylvania German household garden, historically would have a patch of saffron crocus (*Crocus sativus*) *saffran* or *safferich*, a late summer to early autumn blooming corm, each of which bears up to four flowers—each flower has three stigmas, which when dried are the saffron spice. Tedious to harvest, it was often a chore given to children. The corms can be over-planted with summer-blooming annuals like nasturtiums (*Tropaeolum officinale*), grown by the Dutch for their buds that would then be pickled and used as a caper substitute. They also appreciated the beauty of those flowers that were allowed to bloom.

The line between ornamental plants and herbs or even garden crops is not always clear-cut because many attractive plants have had alternative uses. The **BLACKBERRY LILY** (*Belamcanda chinensis*) is a case in point, as the HSP explains:

Originally from Asia, this perennial plant grows to about three feet tall and produces a small, vivid orange, speckled flower. The seedpod of this plant looks like a blackberry. It has been grown at Monticello since 1807. Historically, this plant was used medicinally for sore throats, upset stomach and arrow poisoning, as well as being used as an ornamental. Cold stratification is recommended for approximately two weeks before planting, or plant out in the fall. [Expect the plant to self-sow as well.]

BUTTERFLY WEED (*Asclepia tuberosa*) or *Lunga Graüt* is purely ornamental.

Blackberry lily seeds still attached to the plants' stems.

Butterfly weed seeds are manually separated from their long narrow pods (left).

Considered a perennial, *Asclepias* will produce flowers in its second year of growth, like a biennial. The orange flowers bloom from midsummer to fall and will bring butterflies into your garden. With its long tap root, Butterfly Weed does not like to be transplanted, so pick a sunny location as its permanent spot. It will grow wild as easily as cultivated, thus its lesser known nickname of "railroad Annie." As a member of the milkweed family (to which some gardeners find themselves allergic), the Butterfly Weed produces canoe-shaped seed pods that can be used in dried flower arrangements. This plant emerges late in the spring, so you may want to mark its spot in the garden before it disappears for the winter.

CALENDULA or pot marigold (*Calendula officinalis*), *Ringel Blumm* or *Ringelros* is an all-purpose plant. Beautiful flowers of yellows and oranges make it a garden favorite, but there's more. The plant has been credited with medicinal qualities and the flowers are used as a dyestuff. Additionally, the young leaves are edible as a pot-herb. A hardy annual, it can survive light frosts and early snow. It has been cultivated by mankind for so long that its Old World origins are obscure.

In Africa and parts of Asia the leaves of **CELOSIA** or **COXCOMB** (*Celosia cristata*) are eaten as a cooked vegetable. Among the Dutch *HaahneKamm* is grown as an ornamental prized for its convoluted flowers. After shaking the tiny black seeds from the flowers, the Heirloom Seed Project gardeners divvy up the beautiful wine-colored blooms for use in their dried flower arrangements. The flowers are also naturally occurring in tones of yellow and orange. An associated variety, *Celosia argentea*, is grown for its feathery flowers.

COLUMBINE (*Aguilegia*) is "A pretty garden flower that graced many old gardens," notes the HSP. An often self-seeding perennial, the plant blooms the second year from seed. While the Indians used parts of the plants medicinally, much of it is toxic. The wild columbine of Pennsylvania Dutch country is orange. The Heirloom Seed Project mixture is likely "... to produce pink, rose, dark blue or purple [flowers which] may be accented with white markings."

ELECAMPANE (*Inula helenium*) was first grown as a veterinary medicinal herb and its common English names are scabwort and horseheal. A tall shaggy plant growing up to four feet, it prefers damp shade but can adapt to sun and is grown for its shaggy yellow-to-orange ray flowers that bloom in summer.

FEVERFEW (*Tanacetum parthenium*) was known to the Dutch as *Maederly* and is again a plant of many uses. However, today it is grown essentially as an ornamental for its small white ray flowers with golden centers that were once used as a dyestuff. The aromatic leaves give the plant its name. Brewed into a tea, it was traditionally used to lower fevers. Modern

Young plants being "hardened off" before being sold. Unless properly acclimated to the out-of-doors, young plants are hurt when they come out of the growing house.

clinical tests show this to be a placebo effect, nevertheless modern herbalists credit the plant with medicinal qualities. The HSP's strain dates from prior to 1800.

The traditional pre-1800 **HOLLYHOCK** (*Althea rosea*) or *Halsros* was treasured by the Dutch who often used them in the center bed of four square gardens. Generations of little girls made dolls by inverting the blossoms so that the petals became a "skirt" and the long style became the "body." The HSP describes it:

> Tucked in the corner of your garden or used as a backdrop for your border bed, hollyhock's 3'–9' height ads a regal beauty to any garden. Grow in full sun and well-drained soil. Hollyhocks are susceptible to mildew and should be planted where they can get good air circulation. You may need to stake your plants, but a trellis works just as well and adds a bit more grace to these wonderful biennials.

The **HYACINTH BEAN** (*Lablab purpureus*), a climber, is "a fascinating combination of fragrant, sweet pea-like purple flowers and dark purple seed pods, against deep green and purple/brown foliage," says the HSP. It is a longtime favorite to grow along fences and arbors. Its flowers attract hummingbirds and its leaves are edible and especially enjoyed in some Asian cuisines. The beans are poisonous because of high concentrations of cyanogenic glucosides, but they can be eaten after long boiling and several water changes. The Dutch grew them "just for pretty."

Also grown for its ornamental value is **JOB'S TEARS** (*Coix lachryma Jobi var stenocarpa*), which the Germans called *Karrell* or *FlussKarrell*, an Asian native that grows wild in the South (probably introduced by the Spanish into Florida). Corn-like, the plant is cultivated for its hard-shelled tear-shaped seeds that range in color from pale gray to black. Some Indian tribes used strings of tears as teething rings. The Germans used the beads for jewelry and other ornamental uses. Catholic Germans made rosaries of the seeds. A close relative, *Coix lachryma- Jobi var ma-yuen* is a rice-like grain that can be found in healthfood stores under the name *Hato mungi*.

LARKSPUR (*Delphinium consolida*), *Ritterschpar*, in Dutch, is:

> An absolutely beautiful sight for your eyes in early to mid-summer when your larkspur is in full bloom. Mostly blue with some pink flowers [and white], this flower has dressed gardens since colonial days. Once planted, your larkspur will travel at will throughout your garden from year to year. … Sow in ordinary garden soil in full sun to light, filtered shade. Pretty in bouquets and dried or pressed arrangements. The *Delphinium* genus is considered toxic and should not be used internally and should be kept away from livestock.

LUNARIA (*Lunaria annua*) has many names. The English called it honesty; in continental Europe it became known by some variation of the name *judaspeenning* (coins of Judas.) In America, it is often known as silver dollars or Chinese money. All are names for:

> …this self-sowing biennial that is widely grown for its flat, translucent seed pods that look like silver dollars. In late spring/early summer it treats us to pink-purple, honey scented flowers that resemble Phlox. Seed pods develop in early fall and are used in dry arrangements after the outer membrane and seeds are removed. This reveals the

silvery membrane. Lunaria can be started inside in late spring and transplanted to the garden in mid-summer, or it can be sowed directly into the garden in mid-summer for bloom the following year. It likes full sun to partial shade and can reach heights of 3'.

ROSE CAMPION (*Lychinis coronaria* or *Selene coronaria*) is a short-lived perennial that freely self-seeds. Most commonly a rose magenta flower, a white form is also common. Because of its silvery, wooly leaves, the plant is sometimes called dusty miller. The English often refer to it as bloody William. A well-known garden flower, native to Europe and a relative of the carnation, it has long been a favorite in Pennsylvania German gardens.

SAFFLOWER (*Carthamus tinctorius*) is notorious "... at the Heirloom Seed Project's 'seed house' for the prickly beauty of the seed bract." The pre-1850 seed line resembles baby teeth. It is grown in the garden for its orange to red flowers whose petals are used to add color (if not pseudo-flavor) to foods like noodles instead of the more expensive and favored saffron. Hence the plant is often called American or False Saffron. Growing one to three feet tall, the plant does not transplant well and likes full sun and a well-drained soil. Commercially, fields of it are grown for the seeds that produce safflower oil, a popular, almost tasteless, cooking oil.

THIN-LEAVED CONEFLOWER (*Rudbeckia triloba*) is a pre-1850 garden plant often mistaken for Black-eyed Susan (*Rudbeckia hirta*) but this "happy yellow-orange perennial flower," as the HSP describes it, blooms continuously from summer to fall with smaller, more plentiful flowers. "Don't expect flowers from seed the first year, but after that … wow!"

PASTEL YARROW (*Achillea millefolium cultivars*) are all derived from the species *Achillea*, a white flower type that is native to the northern hemisphere. It is named for the mythological Greek warrior Achilles who, according to legend, carried it into battle to treat wounds. Hence it is also known as herbal militaris. Other names are staunchweed and soldiers woundwort. The HSP's mixture of seeds provide pale yellow to pink blossoms over a long blooming period, which are excellent for cutting.

Safflowers and safflower seeds.

Of course, many other flowers are included in a selection of plants the Pennsylvania Germans favored. A larger list is included in chapter II. Among these are Marigolds, Sweet William, and the Madonna Lily.

The marigold was often known as the French Marigold or the African Marigold. All of these flowers of the genus *Tagetes* are native to the Americas. The term French is generally applied to small-flowered, low-growing flowers (*Tagetes patula*). Larger flowered taller plants are often referred to as African or Mexican (*Tagetes erectra*), but many plants are hybrids of both. *Tagetes* are said to deter nematodes as well as many insects and are therefore widely used as companion plantings for tomatoes, peppers, eggplant, tobacco, and potatoes. Because the roots extrude the antibacterial *thiophenes*, it is not best planted near legumes. Many people find the plant's aroma objectionable; others enjoy it. The Dutch, however, often referred to it as *Stinken* or *Schtinken blumen*.

SWEET WILLIAM (*Dianthus barbatus*) is a beautifully scented member of the carnation family that is an easily grown biennial. To this day it is grown by Pennsylvania German market gardeners in South Central Pennsylvania, A native of southern Europe, the plant was popularized by John Gerard, famed sixteenth-century English herbalist, and it is probably named for William Shakespeare. It is emblematic of the inter-relationship between English and German cultures, both in the homelands but especially in the Pennsylvania German heartland. As a contemporary noted when Catherine Middleton wed Prince William, a descendent of the Hanoverian kings, on April 29, 2011, the flower sweet william, was included in her bouquet.

The **MADONNA LILY** (*Lilium candidum*), a native of the Balkans and West Asia, was the first true lily commonly grown in Pennsylvania German gardens where it was appreciated for its religious associations as well as its beauty and aroma. In the late nineteenth century many lilies were introduced from Asia that were more spectacular and easier to grow—and that eventually supplanted this emblematic flower.

Even in traditional gardens, tended by traditional-minded gardeners, there was always some taste for the new. Accordingly, there is one other topic we haven't yet mentioned – and that is exotic plants. You see **ELEPHANT EARS** (*Colocasia araceae*) everywhere. Even on Amish and Mennonite farms. Photographs show that the Landis family grew **AMARYLLIS**. And going through Dutch country today, you see a wide assortment of unusual plants. Co-author Richman asked his gardening father-in-law about this phenomenon and he recalled the plants from his pre-Depression-era childhood. He related that "…the Dutch always liked odd plants" and he recalled that they got them from "somewhere in the Midwest." And, indeed, there are many seed houses and mail-order nurseries such as Shumway's in Randolph, Wisconsin, in business since 1860, that offer a number of botanical oddities along with plain, everyday beans, peas, and tomatoes. Today's Shumway catalog, still heavily marketed in Dutch Country, features an old-fashioned look emblazoned on the cover with a vignette of a bearded R. H. Shumway described as "The Pioneer American Seedsman." Hyperbole? Perhaps!

The Pennsylvania Germans in their horticulture have always represented a mixture of the old and the new, with the balances shifting with the times. On a summer day in 1914, Henry Harrison Landis noted that he counted more than seventy automobiles passing his farm in a single day. At about the same time he started to lock the chicken house door at night. In the twenty-first century the culture is being diluted as more and more Dutch and their descendents leave the farmland and enter the mainstream. But many of them still garden. Attempting to balance these factors are increasing numbers of preservation, conservation, and cultural organizations and museums. Let us all hope that sustainable new garden and gardening models will be continually reinvented.

V.

The Galleries

of Heirloom Vegetables and Flowers

Balsam apple (*Momordica balsamina*), a relative of the melon, was grown as a curiosity in many gardens. While the fruit is actually poisonous, the pulp was often used as a poultice. It is frequently seen in early American still life paintings. (See James Peale's *Still Life with Balsam Apple* on page 15.) A vigorous vining plant, it also has attractive flowers.

Beans (*Phaseolus vulgaris*) and lima beans (*Phaseolus lunatus*) are among the most popular heirloom crops. Young bean plants emerge in the growing field. Scarlet runner beans are beautiful in flower and produce good beans. Dragon tongues are beautifully marked; the lazy housewife doesn't need shelling; Mostoller wild goose; pole beans grow very long vines; Dr. Martin's pole limas attract a lot of bugs, but give a heavy crop; and harvested seed beans await packing. | *Continued on next page*

PA German Red
Lima Beans

Beet (*Beta vulgaris*). Lutz beets growing and harvested. Deacon Dan beets in flower.

Left | Cabbage (*Brassica oleracea* or variants)—the quintessential Pennsylvania German vegetable.

Right | Cardoon (*Cynara cardunculus*), a relative of the artichoke, is grown for its stalks. An ancient vegetable, it is enjoying a renaissance among foodies. *Lee Stoltzfus.*

Celeriac (*Apium graveolens var. rapaceum*) and celery (*Apium graveolens var. dulce*) are close cousins, one grown as a root, the other for stalks. *Lee Stoltzfus and Mr. and Mrs. Michael B. Emery.*

Left | Cucumbers, pickles (*Cucumis sativus*) are grown on long vines, either on the ground or on supporting frames. Since it is used as the quintessential pickle, it is often referred to by that name. *Mr. and Mrs. Michael B. Emery.*

Right | Corn or maize (*Zea mays*). Seneca corn ready for harvest.

Endive (*Cichorium endivia*) an edible member of the daisy family.

Gourds are all *cucurbitaceae*. Louffa or fuffa gourds (*Luffa aegyptiaca*) is grown for its sponge-like interior. Bottle or birdhouse gourds (*Lagenaria siceraria*) are grown for their long-lasting quality. *Lee Stoltzfus.* (*Louffa*).

Kale (*Brassica oleracea Acephala Group*). An old workhorse vegetable, now grown in many varieties.

Kohlrabi, German turnip, turnip, cabbage (*Brassica oleracea gongylodes*).

Leek (*Allium ampeloprasum*), growing in a raised bed, is a member of the amaryllis family.

Lettuce (*Lactuca sativa*) shares a bed with young brassicas, and is available in many forms.

Mangel, wurzel, or mangel wurzel (*Beta vulgaris var.*), a close relative of the beet, is commonly grown as animal food. Young tender roots were also used as human food on occasion. *Lee Stoltzfus.*

Onions (*Allium cepa*) have wonderful flower-heads that yield abundant seed. The Pennsylvania Dutch Onion is listed in a 1948 catalog. A less common onion, very popular with the Dutch, is the Egyptian or Walking Onion (*Allium x proliferum*), a top-setting perennial onion with a cluster of bulblets developing where regular onions would have flowers. They are especially good for providing season-long green onions. *Onion photographs, Lee Stoltzfus.*

Melons in the Pennsylvania German context mean cantaloupe or muskmelon (*Cucumis malo*), an ancient introduction from India via Europe.

Parsnip (*Pastinaca sativa*) is a root vegetable closely related to the carrot, which can be left in the ground and harvested all winter. *Lee Stoltzfus.*

Peas, sweet peas, English peas, sugar peas (*Pisum sativum*) are, of course, botanically fruits, but a common early vegetable traditionally grown on twig or branch supports.

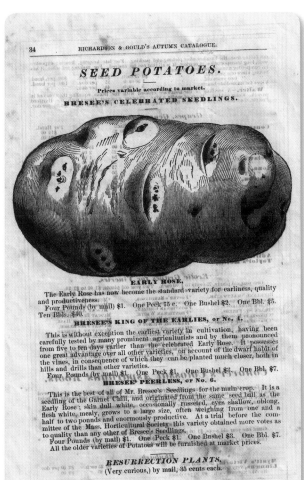

Potatoes (*Solanum brevicaule* complex) exist in over 1,000 varieties. The Early Rose, introduced in the mid-nineteenth century, was grown by Henry H. Landis (1838–1926) on his family farm, now the Landis Valley Village and Farm Museum, for many years. Potatoes in bloom share a vegetable garden.

Pumpkins (*Cucurbita pepo*) come in many shapes and several colors. Common field pumpkins are often used for Jack-o'-lanterns. White ones such as the fortuna (*var. papol*) are primarily used for cooking.

Radishes (*Raphanus sativus*) of many common types are offered in a 1923 seed catalog. The Munchen bier or rat tailed radish (*Raphanus candatus*) is grown for its seed pods, which are historically eaten with beer. These radishes were especially popular in America in the mid-nineteenth century.

Left | Rhubarb or pie plant (*Rheum rhabarbarum*) is grown for its stalks. The lush, inviting-looking leaves are poisonous.

Right | Rye (*Secale cereale*) is grown for its many qualities; the grain is used for bread and whiskey making, the stalks in basket weaving and roof thatching.

Salsify, oyster plant (*Tragopogon porrifolius*) is a dual function plant in the garden. The roots are edible, if difficult to peel, and the flowers and seadheads are very ornamental.

Sorrel, garden sorrel, sourgrass (*Runex acetosa*) is a perennial leaf vegetable prized for its crisp sour flavor.

Squash (*Cucurbita*) are grown in many varieties, both summer and winter. Pictured here are varied winter squash after harvest; pattypan squash growing; and a crook-necked squash patch the morning after the season's first frost.

Left | Sweet potatoes, yams (*ipomoea batatas*) are the roots of a vining member of the morning glory family. Whether orange, yellow or red, our favored Thanksgiving side dish is often erroneously called a yam, which is in fact an entirely different tropical root of the genus *Dioscorea*.

Right | Swiss chard (*Beta vulgaris subsp. Cicia*), both red and yellow stemmed, grows in a raised bed.

Tomatoes (*Solanum lycopersicum* formerly *lycopersicon esculentum*) is our most popular heirloom plant, one available in hundreds of varieties. Most are grown from young plants transplanted into the garden or the growing field. As they develop, tomato plants are not always a joy to the eye, even if they are producing a bountiful crop. In varied photogenic states several varieties including Amish paste, German strawberry, and Brandywine appear before the camera.

Black Brandywine, pepper, and Hartman yellow gooseberry fruits pose after being picked.

Turnip (*Brassica rapifera*) was a more popular vegetable in past years, especially because of its keeping qualities. In flower, as seen in this four square garden, the plants can be sensational.

Watermelon (*Citrullus lanatus*) is originally from Africa and may have come into America with African slaves. While it thrives in the South it was also commonly grown in parts of the North. Popular with the Pennsylvania Germans was the interestingly marked "Moon and Stars" variety.

A GALLERY OF HEIRLOOM FLOWERS AND HERBS

Left | Amaranth (*Amaranthus*) in several varieties has long been grown as an ornamental prized for catkin-like cymes of densely packed flowers and often variegated leaves. Its variants have many fanciful popular names including "My Love Lies Bleeding" and "Kiss Me Quick Over the Fence." Amaranth seeds are used as a grain in many cultures and are familiar to gluten adverse Americans today. *Lee Stoltzfus.*

Right | Angelica, garden Angelica (*Angelica archangelica*) was photographed growing in Alsace. The Germans candied young stalks and used the leaves as a seasoning. *Lee Stoltzfus.*

Giant Emperor Aster.

Left | Aster, China aster (*Callistephus chinensis*) were very popular in the nineteenth and early twentieth centuries for their full flowers and broad color range. Gardens also included New England asters (*Symphyotrichum novae-angliae*), single blooms borne in clusters, which, as the name suggests, is an American native.

Arums (*Arum dracunculus*) and *Arum italicum* were common garden plants. They are close relatives of the jack-in-the-pulpit (*Arisaema triphyllum*), an American native. This illustration is from an 1871 catalog.

Below | Basil, sweet basil (*Ocimum basilicum*) comes in many variants. Young plants await the Landis Valley Herb and Garden Faire in a hoop house.

Bachelor's button, cornflower (*Centaurea cyanus*) was prized for its blue color but scorned as a weed in grain fields.

Blackberry lily, leopard flower (*Iris domestica* formerly *Belamcanda chinensis*) is grown both for its spotted orange flowers and its clusters of black seeds that appear berry-like. A perennial member of the iris family, it seeds itself freely.

Bears breeches (*Acanthus balcanicus*) is a perennial prized for its tropical-appearing leaves and attractive floral spikes. *Lee Stoltzfus*.

Bleeding heart (*Lamprocapnos spectabilis* formerly *Dicentra spectabilis*) is an Asian plant first introduced into England in the 1840s and which soon crossed the Atlantic. By the 1870s it became a beloved common garden flower in the Eastern United States. *Lee Stoltzfus*.

Bloodroot (*Sanguinaria canadensis*), native to the eastern United States, was prized for its medicinal qualities by the Native Americans as well as the Europeans. It, along with another American native, the yellow-flowered greater celandine poppy *(Chelidonium majus)*, was used to cure warts. It can be toxic. *Lee Stoltzfus*.

Burnet or salad burnet (*Sanguisorba minor*) is a central European native that has naturalized in much of North America. Its leaves are used in salads and dressings—often described as light cucumber or celery-like flavor—depending on your palate. It is often combined in traditional dishes with borage flowers (*Borago officinalis*).

Calendula, pot marigold (*Calendula officinalis*) plants are shown at the Herb and Garden Faire. A multifaceted plant, its young leaves are a "pot herb" or a cooking green. The yellow and orange ray flowers are prized for their beauty and as a dyestuff.

Castor bean plant, castor oil plant (*Ricinus communis*) is prized as a fast-growing ornamental but the entire plant, and especially the beans, is toxic. Properly handled the beans are the source of castor oil, a widely used medicinal into the mid-twentieth century, but the plant also contains ricin, a deadly poison. *Lee Stoltzfus.*

Oenothera (*Oenothera macrocarpa*) is a perennial grown for its showy flowers. *Lee Stoltzfus.*

Chamomile, German chamomile, or scented mayweed (*Matricaria recutita* also known as *Matricaria chamomilla*) are the common names for a daisy-like plant that has been made into a tea for millennia. It is valued for its soothing qualities, but today it is known that it can cause miscarriage and, if you are allergic to ragweed, you might have a problem with chamomile as well. *Flowers, Lee Stoltzfus.*

Chives (*Allium schoenoprasum*) growing in the Show Garden at the Landis Valley Village and Farm Museum, is the only member of the onion or allium family native to both Europe and North America.

Cleome, spider flower, bee plant (*Cleome hassleriana*) is a native of South America and a northern garden staple since the eighteenth century.

Comfrey (*Symphytum officinale*) has large hairy leaves and blue flowers and a long tradition of use as a folk remedy. It is still in use as a skin treatment but has been banned by the FDA for internal use. Its leaves, however, have another use—as an organic fertilizer.

D-528   COTTON BLOSSOMS IN DIXIELAND

E-5407

Cosmos, garden cosmos (*Cosmos bipinnatus*) is native to Mexico. A member of the *Asteraceae* family, it is an easy to grow annual, very free in its seed production. It ranges from white to pink to purple-red. An allied plant also grown is chocolate cosmos (*Cosmos atrosanguineus*) available in yellows through browns. *Lee Stoltzfus.*

Cotton (*Gossypium hirsutum*) is a southern crop, but in southcentral Pennsylvania and Maryland a few plants were grown as a garden ornamental for the attractive flowers—and a bonus, heads of cotton—if you were lucky. *The Cottage Collection.*

Crocus, crocuses (*Crocus ligusticus*), is a large family of European bulbs, long in cultivation. The mammoth yellow is an old favorite. The oldest crocus generally found in Dutch areas is *Crocus tommasinianus* or *"tommies,"* a small lavender-flowered plant. *Lee Stoltzfus.*

Daffodils, narcissus, jonquils (*Narcissus*), are a large complex group of Old World bulbs. These bi-colored blossoms were photographed on an Old Order Amish farm in Lancaster County. *Lee Stoltzfus.*

Dame's rocket, sweet rocket (*Hesperis matronalis*), in the mustard family, is a biennial with very free seed production. It has become a wildflower in many areas.

Above & below | Dill (*Anethum graveolens*) is a dramatic herb, often towering over other garden plants. It is seen here growing behind the Robert Fulton birthplace in Lancaster County, Pennsylvania, and with a costumed interpreter at Old Salem, North Carolina. *Old Salem photograph, Lee Stoltzfus.*

Flax (*Linum usitatissimum*) is a field crop that produces fiber (linen) as well as seeds used for producing linseed oil. Small stands were grown in gardens for their beautiful blue blossoms. There are several linums or flaxes grown primarily as garden ornamentals, including perennial blue flax (*Linum perenne*), scarlet flax (*L. grandiflorum*), and golden flax (*L. flavum*).

Forget-me-not (*Myosotis arvensis*) is a sentimental self-seeding annual and a popular emblem used on greeting cards and scrapbook images. *The Cottage Collection.*

Ginger, wild ginger (*Asarum canadense*) is grown for its beautiful leaves and unusual blossoms. Its tubers smell like the spice ginger, (*Zingiber officinale*), an Asian plant. An allied plant, European Ginger, or wild European ginger (*Asarum europaeum*) is also grown in gardens.

Gladioli, gladiolus (*Gladiolus angustus*) are popular summer flowers grown from corms. The Pennsylvania Dutch artist Charles Demuth (1883–1935) painted flowers from his mother's traditional garden.

Left | Hollyhock (*Alcea rosea*) is the ultimate cottage flower and was occasionally used in the center bed of German four square gardens. *Lee Stoltzfus.*

Right | Hops are the female flowers of the hop plant (*Humulus lupulus*) that were grown as ornamentals, but especially for use in beer and bread making.

Horehound (*Marrubium vulgare*) is used to flavor candies and as a medicinal. *Flowers, Lee Stoltzfus.*

Horseradish (*Armoracia rusticana*) root provides
the most popular traditional condiment.

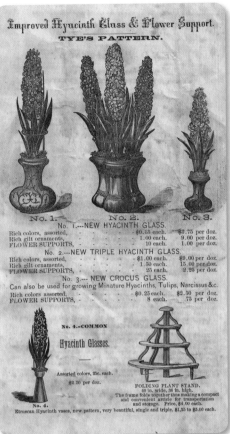

Hyacinth (*Hyacinthus orientalis*) was a popular
plant for both garden use and for forcing in
"Hyacinth Glasses." The grape hyacinth is a
Muscari and not related to the true hyacinth.

Hyacinth bean (*Lablab purpureus*), formally
Dolichos lablab, is prized as an ornamental.
While the flowers and the leaves can be eaten
raw the beans are poisonous unless boiled, with
several water changes.

Impatience, zanzibar balsam, bizzy lizzy
(*Impatiens walleriana*) is a pre-hybridized
ancestor of our familiar bedding plant.

Iris (*Iris germanica*) is a very large family of flowers. Most commonly the Pennsylvania Germans grew a class
of bearded iris (*germanica*) that you still see everywhere. *Lee Stoltzfus.*

Job's Tears

(Coix Lachryma)

Seeds Can Be Used As Beads

This interesting ornamental grass is chiefly grown for the seeds which resemble beads. In grandmother's days it was used as a remedy for sore-throat and teething babies, being strung on a linen thread and worn around the neck.

No. 2486, Pkt. 10c; oz. 25c; 4 ozs. 75c.

GOOD LUCK GARDENS

Larkspur (*Delphinium consolida*) is a free-seeding annual.

Lamb's ear (*Stachys byzantina*), a perennial, is a native of Turkey. In a more modern parlance it is occasionally called "Scouting toilet paper" because its leaves are soft and hairy. *Lee Stoltzfus.*

Job's tears, tear grass (*Coix lacryma-jobi*) is grown for its seeds, which are used in making ornaments and jewelry.

Lemon balm (*Melissa officinalis*) is a vigorous self-seeding perennial member of the mint family widely used as a tea.

LILIUM AURATUM.

THE GOLDEN RAYED QUEEN OF LILIES.

Large Flowering Bulbs, ... 35 cents to $1.00 each.

Lily of the valley (*Convallaria majalis*) is prized for its sweet-smelling flowers. Plants are offered for sale at the Landis Valley Herb and Garden Faire. *Flowers, The Cottage Collection.*

Lilies (*Lilium*) have long been favorites. The Madonna lily (*Lilium candidum*) is the most ancient. After 1860 Asian blooms such as *Lilium auratum* became popular. Daylilies (*Heemerocallis flava*), not true lilies, were also often grown and called "lilies."

Lobelia, Indian tobacco (*Lobelia inflata*) is an herbal remedy used for many ailments. A close relative Cardinal Flower (*Lobelia cardinalis)* with scarlet blossoms was also grown. *Lee Stoltzfus.*

Lovage (*Levisticum officinale*) is a tall perennial whose leaves are prized for their celery-like flavor. *Lee Stoltzfus.*

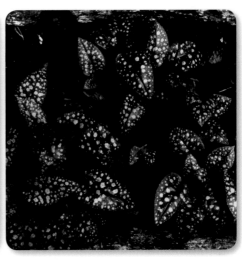

Lungwort (*Pulmonaria saccharata*) is grown for its attractive spotted leaves and its flowers. Historically, teas made from it were used to treat lung ailments. *Lee Stoltzfus.*

Lupine (*Lupinus polyphyllus*) is a popular garden plant that also becomes a wilding under the right conditions.

Mint, tea (*Mentha*) is an enormous family. Many varieties are grown in old gardens or meadows, especially peppermint (*Mentha piperita*) and spearmint (*Mentha spicata*). *Lee Stoltzfus.*

Mole plant, gopher spurge (*Euphorbia lathyris*) is believed to keep moles out of your garden.

Monarda, scarlet beebalm, Oswego tea, bergamot (*Monarda didyma*) is grown as an ornamental and as a tea plant. *Lee Stoltzfus.*

Morning glory (*Ipomoea tricolor*) is a popular summer flower. 'Heavenly Blue' has been extensively grown since the nineteenth century. *William Ames LaFond.*

Mullein, great mullein (*Verbascum thapsus*) is a medicinal herb used for coughs and skin ailments. It self-seeds and can quickly become a weed. The leaves can be mistaken for those of lamb's ears, but they are irritating! *Lee Stoltzfus.*

Left & right | Nasturtium, Indian cress (*Tropaeolum majus*), is seen in a growing house and in the garden.

Obedient plant, false dragonhead (*Physostegia virginiana*), an American native whose flower head can be bent and will keep its shape.

Oenothera, evening primrose, sun drop (*Oenothera biennis*) is a North American native. *Lee Stoltzfus.*

Parsley (*Petroselinum crispum*) in young plants
and in bloom.

Pansy (*Viola x wittrockiana*), seen in an early
twentieth-century postcard, has been a
longtime favorite. A close relative of the violet, or
viola (*Viola sororia*), pansies were considered a
springtime flower. The sweet violet (*Viola
odorata*) was also prized. *The Cottage Collection.*

Peony, fern leaf peony, (*Paeonia tenuifolia*) is
an old variety widely grown in early gardens.
It has mostly been overtaken in popularity by
the more familiar large-flowered herbaceous
peonies like *P. lactiflora* and *P. japonica.*
Lee Stoltzfus.

Phlox (*Phlox*) is grown in four types: wild or woods *P. divaricata*; *P. stolonifera*; creeping phlox, *P.
subulata* (pictured) and garden phlox, *P. paniculata*, which is seen in this icirca 1870 nursery book,
sample plate published in Rochester, New York, by Dellon Marcus Dewey. *Photograph, Lee Stoltzfus;
sample plate, The Cottage Collection.*

Pink, maiden pink (*Dianthus deltoides*) is a common old garden perennial of the carnation family. It is a close relative to the biennial sweet william (*Dianthus barbatus*), which has been grown in America since the seventeenth century. *Lee Stoltzfus.*

Poppy (*Papaver somniferum*) is a beautiful flower, one of a number in its family. *P. somniferum* has edible seeds and opium can also be extracted from the pods. Close relatives include the Iceland poppy (*Papaver nudicaule*) and Oriental poppy (*Papaver orientale*).

Rose campion (*Lychnis coronaria*) is a many-branched freely seeding biennial. It has silvery leaves and white, rose or magenta flowers and is an emblematic cottage garden plant.

Rue (*Ruta graveolens*) is a blue-leaved herb grown as a bitter tea and for medicinal purposes.

Safflower (*Carthamus tinctorius*) grows in the Landis Valley Show Garden. It is a thistle-like annual prized as a dyestuff and cooking oil source.

Sage (*Salvia officinalis*) is a common seasoning, necessary in Pennsylvania German sausage. It is a close relative of the garden flower scarlet sage (*S. splendens*).

Left | Southernwood, lad's love, southern wormwood (*Artemisia abrotanum*) is used as a dye plant and an insect repellent.

Right | Sunflowers (*Helianthus atrorubens*) grow in a garden near the Stone Tavern. This old-fashioned variety was favored for its long blooming season and cheerful color and hues. *Landis Valley Village and Farm Museum, Craig Benner photographer.*

Schwartzbeeren, garden huckleberry is an edible black nightshade introduced by the Volga Germans in the Midwest in the 1870s that found its way into Pennsylvania. Parts of the plant are toxic and it is closely allied to the poisonous variant. *Lee Stoltzfus.*

Tansy, cow bitter (*Tanacetum vulgare*) has a long history as a medicinal herb and an insect repellent. *Lee Stoltzfus.*

Tithonia, Mexican sunflower (*Tithonia rotundifolia*) is easy to grow from seed and it is outstanding in seed production.

Tulip (*Tulipa gesneriana*) has been a favored bulb since the earliest colonial period. It is available in many forms and colors, except for blue and black. *Yellow Flowers; Lee Stoltzfus.*

Valerian, garden valerian (*Valeriana officinalis*) is an attractive plant but it was mostly grown for its root, which yields a sedative. *In flower, Lee Stoltzfus.*

Veronica, speedwell (*Veronica americana*) is an edible pot herb and was used by Native Americans to brew a tea used to alleviate bronchial congestion.

Yarrow (*Achillea millefolium*) is grown medicinally to treat wounds, but most commonly, it is favored as a garden perennial requiring little water. *Lee Stoltzfus.*

A LOVE FOR EXOTICS

Tree peony (*Paeonia suffruticosa*), a nineteenth century introduction from China, dominates a carefully tended backyard garden in Glen Rock, York County, Pennsylvania, circa 1900.

George Diller, the maternal grandfather of George and Henry Landis, founders of the Landis Valley Museum, sits on his porch on a summer day around 1890 surrounded by tender houseplants summering out-of-doors. *Henry K. Landis.*

Houseplants summer on a bench behind a young girl pictured on a circa 1910 postcard. *The Cottage Collection.*

The Pennsylvania Germans prized redware flowerpots. Elaborate ones were common gifts to mark life's milestones.

A white-bearded gentleman waters his exuberant cottage garden, around 1915.

AN ENDNOTE

Everything old in the gardening sphere is new.
Only the price is modern on this reproduction of
a turn-of-the-century Hart Seed packet, packed
for 2013. *The Cottage Collection.*

APPENDIX A

HERITAGE GARDENS, GARDEN SITES AND HERITAGE LANDSCAPE

While we have made this list as accurate as possible, hours have a way of shifting.

Always double-check by phone or website before visiting.

1719 Hans Herr House
1849 Hans Herr Drive, Willow Street, PA 17584
Phone: (717) 464-4438
Web: hansherr.org
Hours: Open April to first week in December.
    Mon.–Sat., 9 a.m.–4 p.m. Admission fee.

Bartram's Gardens
54th Street and Lindbergh Boulevard, Philadelphia,
    PA 19143
Phone: (215) 729-5281
Web: bartramsgarden.org
Hours: Open March–December. Tues.–Fri.,
    noon–4 p.m.; Sat.–Sun., 10 a.m.–5 p.m.
    January and February by appointment.
    Admission fee.

Bowman's Hill Wildflower Preserve
1635 River Road (Pennsylvania 32), New Hope,
    PA 18938
Phone: (215) 862-2924
Web: bhwp.org
Hours: Mon.–Sat., 9 a.m.–5 p.m.; Sun., noon–3
    p.m. Admission fee.

Burnside Plantation
1461 Schoenersville Road, Bethlehem, PA 18018
Phone: (610) 868-5044
Web: historicbethlehem.org
Hours: Open July and August. Sat., noon–4 p.m.,
    and by appointment. Admission fee.

Christ Lutheran Church – Cemetery
36 Main Street, Stouchsburg, PA
Hours: Open daily. No admission fee.

Colonial Industrial Quarter
459 Old York Road, Bethlehem, PA 18018
Phone: (610) 883-0450
Web: historicbethlehem.org
Hours: The grounds are open all year and are
    free of admission charge. Buildings: Summer,
    Thurs.–Sun, noon–4 p.m.. Open March–
    Thanksgiving, Thurs.–Sat., 10 a.m.–5 p.m.;
    Sun., noon–5 p.m. Admission fee.

Colonial Pennsylvania Plantation
3900 North Sandy Flash Drive, Newtown
    Square, PA
Phone: (610) 566-1725
Web: colonialplantation.org
Hours: Sat.–Sun., 11 a.m.–5. Admission fee.

Colonial Williamsburg
134 N. Henry Street, Williamsburg, VA 23187
Phone: (757) 229-1000
Web: colonialwilliamsburg.org
Hours: Open daily. 9 a.m.–5 p.m. Admission fee.

Conrad Weiser Homestead
28 Weiser Lane, Womelsdorf, PA 19567
Phone:(610) 589-2934
Web: *conradweiserhomestead.org*
Hours: In flux. Grounds open daily. House: Every
    Sun. from June to Labor Day. Noon to 4 p.m.
    Admission fee.

Ephrata Cloister
632 W. Main Street, Ephrata, PA 17522
Phone: (717) 733-6600
Web: ephratacloister.org

Hours: Jan.–Feb.: Tues.–Sat., 9 a.m.–5 p.m., Sun.
    noon–5 p.m.. March–Dec,: Mon.–Sat. 9
    a.m.–5 p.m., Sun. noon–5 p.m. Admission fee.

Falkner Swamp U. C. Church Cemetery
2077 Swamp Pike, Gilbertville, Pa 19525
Phone: (610) 323-4053
Web: www.falknerswamp.org
Hours: Grounds open daily. Admission is free.

Frontier Culture Museum of Virginia
1290 Richmond Avenue Staunton, VA 24401
Phone: (546) 332-7850
Web: frontiermuseum.org
Hours: Open mid-March to mid-December,
    daily, 9 a.m.–5 p.m. Mid-Dec to mid-March,
    daily, 10 a.m.–4 p.m. Admission fee.

**Gates House and Golden Plough Tavern,
    Barnett Bobb Log House (Colonial
    Complex)**
157 West market St., York, PA 17403
Phone: (717) 845-2951
Web: www.yorkheritage.org
Hours: Tues.–Sat. tours, 10 a.m.–3 p.m.
    Admission Fee.

Grumblethorpe
5267 Germantown Avenue, Philadelphia, PA 19144
Phone: (215) 843-4820
Web: grumblethorpe@philalandmarks.org
Hours: By appointment. Admission fee.

Harmony Museum
218 Mercer Street, Harmony, PA 16037
Phone: (724) 452-7341
Web: harmonymuseum.org
Hours: Tues.–Sun., 1 p.m.–4 p.m. Admission fee.

Henry Antes Plantation
318 Colonial Road, Perkiomenville, PA 18074
Phone: (215) 234.8953
Web: goschenhoppen.org
Hours: By appointment. Admission fee.

Historic Bethabara Park
2147 Bethabara Road, Winston–Salem, NC 27106
Phone: (336) 924-8191
Web: bethabarapark.org
Hours: Visitor Center and Buildings open April 1– December 12. Tues.–Fri., 10:30 a.m.–4:30; Sat.–Sun, 1:30 p.m.–4:30 p.m. Admission is free.

Historic Preservation Trust of Berks County
31 Old Philadelphia Pike, Douglasville, PA 19518
Phone: (610) 385-4762
Web: historicpreservationtrust.org

Historic Rittenhouse Town
206 Lincoln Drive, Philadelphia, PA 19144
Phone: (215) 438-5711
Web: rittenhousetown.org
Hours: Spring/Summer weekends, 1 p.m.–5 p.m.; Fall/Winter, by appointment. Admission fee.

Historic Schaefferstown, Inc.
106 N. Market Street, Schaefferstown, PA 17088
Phone: (717) 949-2444
Web: www.hsimuseum.org
Hours: April–October, second and fourth Saturdays, 1 p.m.–4 p.m. Admission fee.

The Landis Valley Village and Farm Museum
2451 Kissel Hill Road, Lancaster, PA 17601
Phone: (717) 569-0401 x216
website: www.LandisValleyMuseum.org
Hours: Mon.–Sat., 9 a.m.–5 p.m.; Sun., noon–5 p.m. Winter hours vary. Admission fee.

Lititz Historical Museum and the Johannes Mueller House
137 E. Main Stret, Lititz, PA 17543
Phone: (717) 627-4636
Web: lititzhistoricalfoundation.com
Hours: Memorial Day to last Saturday in October: Mon.–Sat., 10 a.m.–4 p.m.. November to Sat. before Christmas: Fri. and Sat., 10 a.m.–4 p.m.. Admission fee for Mueller House.

Monticello
See **Thomas Jefferson's Monticello**

Moravian Historical Society
214 E. Center Street, Nazareth, PA 18064
Phone: (610) 759-5070
Web: moravianhistoricalsociety.org
Hours: Open daily. 1 p.m.–4 p.m. Admission fee.

Moravian Museum of Bethlehem, Inc.
66 West Church Street, Bethlehem, PA 18018
Phone: (610) 867-0173
Web: historicbethlehem.org
Hours: March to Thanksgiving: Thurs. to Sat., 10 a.m.–5 p.m.; Sun., noon–5 p.m.. Christmas Season: Mon.–Sat., 10 a.m.–5 p.m.; Sun, noon–5 p.m. Admission fee.

Morris Arboretum of the University of Pennsylvania
100 Northwestern Avenue, Philadelphia, PA 19118
Phone: (215) 247-5777
Web: business-services.upenn.edu/arboretum
Hours: Open daily except major holidays. Daily, 10 a.m.–4 except April–October weekends open until 5 p.m., and June–August Thursdays open to 8:30 p.m. Admission fee.

Mount Cuba Center
3120 Barley Mill Road, Hockessin, DE 19707
Phone: (302) 239-4244
Web: mtcubacenter.org
Hours: Season varies; usually mid-April through early November. Sat.–Sun., 10 a.m.–4 p.m. Other times by appointment. Admission fee.

Old Economy Village
270 Sixteenth Street, Ambridge, PA 15003
Phone: (724) 266-4500
Web: oldeconomyvillage.org
Hours: Visitor Center, year-round, Tues.–Sat., 10 a.m.–5 p.m., with extended hours Wed. and Thurs. to 8. Also, every second Sunday, noon–5 p.m. Old Economy Village historic site open on same daily schedule April 1–December 31. Site and visitor center closed all other Sunday, Mondays and major holidays. Admission fee.

Old Salem Museums and Gardens
900 Old Salem Road, Winston–Salem, NC 27108
Phone: (336) 721-7300
Web: oldsalem.org
Hours: Tues.–Sat., 9:30 a.m.–4:30 p.m.; Sun., 1–4:30 p.m. Admission fee.

Pennsbury Manor
400 Pennsbury Memorial Road, Morrisville, PA 19067
Phone: (215) 946-0400
Web: pennsburymanor.org
Hours: Tues.–Sat., 9 a.m.–5 p.m.; Sun., noon–5 p.m. Admission fee.

Pennypacker Mills
5 Haldeman Road Schwenksville, PA 19473
Phone: (610) 287-9349
Web: montcopa.org
Hours: Tues.–Sat., 10 a.m.–4 p.m.; Sun., 1–4 p.m. Suggested donation requested.

Pennsylvania Hospital Physic Garden
9th and Pine Streets, Philadelphia, PA 19167
Phone: (215) 829-3971

Web: uphs.upenn.edu/paharc
Hours: Open daily, dawn to dusk. Free admission.

Peter Wentz Farmstead
2100 Schultz Road, Worcester, PA 19490
Phone: (610) 584-5104
Web: montcopa.org
Hours: Tues.–Sat., 10–4 p.m.; Sun., 1–4 p.m. Last tour, 3:30 p.m. Suggested donation requested.

Quiet Valley Living Historical Farm
347 Quiet Valley Road, Stroudsburg, PA 18360
Phone: (570) 992-6161
Web: quietvalley.org
Hours: June 20 to Labor Day, Tues.–Sat.,10 a.m.–5 p.m.; Sun. 1–5 p.m. Admission fee.

Renfrew Museum and Park
1010 East Market Street, Waynesboro, PA
Phone: (717) 762-0373
Web: renfrewmuseum.org
Hours: House and museum Tues.–Fri., noon–4; Sat. and Sun, 1 p.m.–4 p.m. Admission fee. Park open from dawn to dusk every day. Admission to the park is free.

Schifferstadt Architectural Museum
1110 Rosemont Avenue Frederick, MD 21701
Phone: (301) 663-3885
Web: FrederickCountyLandmarksFoundation.org
Hours: Open April to mid-December. Thurs.–Sun, noon–4 p.m. Admission fee.

Stenton
4601 N 18th Street Philadelphia, PA 19140
Phone: (215) 329-7312
Web: stenton.org
Hours: April to December 23: Tues.–Sat., 1 p.m.–4 p.m. Closed December 24–January 1. Open January to March by appointment. Admission fee.

Thomas Jefferson's Monticello
931 Thomas Jefferson Pkwy, Charlottesville, VA 22902
Phone: (434) 984-9800
Web: www.monticello.org
Hours: Open daily, except Christmas, gates open 8:30 a.m. –6:00 p.m. Admission fee.

Wagner Ritter House and Garden
418 Broad Street, Johnstown, PA 15906
Phone: (814) 539-1889
Web: jaha.org
Hours: April 1–May 31: Sat. and Sun., noon–5. p.m. June 1–October 31, Wed.–Sun., noon–5 p.m. Admission fee.

Wyck
6016 Germantown Avenue Philadelphia, PA 19144
Phone: (215) 848-1690
Web: wyck.org
Hours: Open April 2–Dec 14. Tues., Thurs., and Sat., 1 p.m.–4 p.m. Admission fee.

APPENDIX B

HEIRLOOM SEED SOURCES

Amishland Heirloom Seeds
P.O. Box 365, Reamstown, PA. 17567-0365
Web: www.amishlandseeds.com

Baker Creek Heirloom Seeds
2278 Baker Creek Rd., Mansfield, MO 65704
Web: www.rareseeds.com

W. Atlee Burpee and Company
300 Park Ave., Warminster, PA 18974
Phone: (800) 888-1447
Web: www.burpee.com

Cook's Garden
P.O. Box C5030, Warminster, PA 18974
Phone:(800) 457-9703
Web: www.cooksgarden.com

Fedco Seeds, Inc.
P.O. Box 520, Waterville, ME 04903
Phone: (207) 426-9900
Web: www.fedcoseeds.com

Granny's Heirloom Seeds
P.O. Box 284, Bolivar, MO 65613
Phone: (417) 413-3740
Web: www.grannysheirloomseeds.com

Charles C. Hart Seed Co.
304 Main St., Wethersfield, CT 06109
Phone: (800) 326 HART (4278)
Web: hartseed.com

Heirloom Seed Project
Landis Valley Village and Farm Museum
2451 Kissel Hill Rd., Lancaster, PA 17604
Phone: (717) 569-0401
Web: www.landisvalleymuseum.org

Johnny's Selected Seeds
955 Benton Ave., Winslow, ME 04901
Phone: (207) 861-3000
Web: www.johnnyseeds.com

J. W. Jung Seed Co.
335 S. High St., Randolph, WI 53957
Phone: (800) 247-5864
Web: www.jungseed.com

D. Landreth Seed Company
P. O. Box 165, Sharon Springs, NY 13459
Phone: (800) 342-9461
Web: www.landrethseeds.com

My Patriot Supply
4201 N. Old State Rd 3, Muncie, IN 47303
Phone: (866) 229-0927
Web: www.mypatriotsupply.com

Old Salem Museums and Gardens
600 South Main St., Winston-Salem, NC 27101
Phone: (336)721-7300
Web: www.oldsalem.org

Organic Heirloom Plants
51594 Boston Rd., Hancock, MI 49930
Phone: (906) 482-0342
Web: www.organicheirloomplants.com

Park Seed Company
3507 Cokesbury Rd., Hodges, SC
Phone: (800) 845-3369
Web: www.parkseed.com

Pinetree
P. O. Box 300
New Gloucester, ME 04260
Phone: (207) 926-3400
Web: www.superseeds.com

Reimer Seeds
P.O. Box 236, Mt. Holly, NC 28120
Web: www.reimerseeds.com

Renee's Garden Seeds
6060 Graham Hill Rd., Felton, CA 95018
Phone: (888) 880-7228
Web: www.reneesgarden.com

Rohrer Seeds
2472 Old Philadelphia Pike, Smoketown, PA
    17576
Phone: (717) 299-2571
Web: www.rohrerseeds.com

Seed Savers Exchange
3094 North Winn Rd., Decorah, IA 52101
Phone: (563) 382-5990
Web: www.seedsavers.org

Seeds n Such
P.O. Box 1, Graniteville, SC 29829
Phone: (888) 474-4010
Web: www.SeedsNSuch.com

Seeds of Change
P.O. Box 4908, Rancho Domingues, CA 90220
Phone: (888)762-7333
Web: www.seedsofchange.com

Select Seeds
180 Stickney Hill Rd., Union, CT 06076
Phone:(800) 684-0395
Web: www.selectseeds.com

John Sheepers Kitchen Garden Seeds
23 Tulip Drive, Bantam, CT 06750
Phone: (860) 567-6086
Web: www.kitchengardenseeds.com

R. H. Shumway's
383 West Second St., Randolph, WI 53956
Phone: (800) 342-9461
Web: www.rhshumway.com

Solana Seeds
17 place Leger, Repentigny, Quebec, Canada
    J6A 5N7
Web: http://solanaseeds.netfirms.com/

Southern Exposure
P.O. Box 460, Mineral, VA 23117
Phone: (540) 894-9480
Web: www.southernexposure.com

Stokes Seed Company
P.O. Box 548, Buffalo, NY 14240
Phone: (800) 263-7233
Web: www.stokeseeds.com

Sustainable Seed Company
P.O. Box 38, Covelo CA, 95428
Phone: (877) 620-SEED
Web: www.sustainableseedco.com

Territorial Seed Company
P.O. Box 158, Cottage Grove, OR 97424
Phone: (800) 626-0866
Web: www.territorialseed.com

Thomas Etty Esq.
Seedsman's Cottage, Puddlebridge, Horton,
    Ilminster, Somerset, TA19 9RL, United Kingdom
Phone: +44(0) 01460 298249
Web: www.thomasetty.co.uk

Thomas Jefferson's Monticello
931 Thomas Jefferson Pkwy, Charlottesville, VA
    22902
Phone: (434) 984-9800
Web: www.monticelloshop.org

Totally Tomatoes
334 West Stroud St., Randolph, WI 53956
Phone: (800) 345-5977
Web: www.totallytomato.com

Vermont Bean Seed Company
334 W. Stroud St., Randolph, WI 53956
Phone: (800) 349-1071
Web: www.vermontbean.com

SOURCES AND SUGGESTIONS
FOR ADDITIONAL READING

Root Crops. Scranton, Pennsylvania: International Correspondence School, n.d.

Adams, Denice Wiles. *Restoring American Gardens: An Encyclopedia of Heirloom Ornamental Plants, 1640–1940.* Portland, Oregon: Timber Press, 2004.

Ash, Thomes. *Carolina, or a Description of the Present State of That Country, etc.* London, 1682 : N.P.

Ashworth, Susan. *Seed to Seed: Seed Saving and Growing Techniques for Vegetable Growers.* Second edition. Decorah, Iowa: Seed Savers Exchange, 2002.

Banks, Elizabeth. *Creating Period Gardens.* Washington, DC: Preservation Press, 1991.

Berger, Terry. "'Tulipiana' was No Dutch Treat to Gambling Burghers." *Smithsonian Magazine* (April 1977): 70–77.

Berkeley, Edmund and Dorothy Smith Berkeley. *The Life and Travels of John Bartram: From Lake Ontario to the River St. John.* Tallahassee, Florida: University Press of Florida, 1990.

Boyd, Karen Kumler. "Pennsylvania German Gardens." *Lancaster* [Pennsylvania] *New Era* (March 25, 1988): 17.

Bubel, Nancy. *The New Seed Starter's Handbook.* Emmaus, Pennsylvania: Rodale Press, 1988.

Cook, Jack. "Rounding Up Jacob's Cattle: The Heirloom-Bean Business." *Horticulture* (July 1982): 11–17.

Coulter, Lynn. *Gardening with Heirloom Seeds: Tried and True.* Chapel Hill, North Carolina: University of North Carolina Press, 2006.

D. Landreth Seed Company. *Heirloom Bulb Collection: Garlic & Flowers.* New Freedom, Pennsylvania: D. Landreth Seed Company, 2012.

Dunmire, William W. *Gardens of New Spain: How Mediterranean Plants and Foods Changed America.* Austin, Texas: University of Texas Press, 2004.

Dutton, Joan Perry. *Plants of Colonial Williamsburg.* Williamsburg, Virginia: The Colonial Williamsburg Foundation, 1979.

Emery, Michael B. and Irwin Richman. *Yesterday's Farm Tools and Equipment: Featuring Collections of the Landis Valley Museum.* Atglen, Pennsylvania: Schiffer Publishing. 2010.

Eyler, Ellen G. *Early English Gardens and Garden Books,* Ithaca, New York: Cornell University Press, and Washington, DC: Folger Shakespeare Press, 1963.

Favretti, Rudy J. and Joy P. Favretti. *For Every House a Garden: A Guide for Reproducing Period Gardens.* Lebanon, N.H.: University Press of New England, 1990.

Fielding, Burr. *Field and Garden Vegetables of America,* reprint of 1863, third ed. Chillicothe, Illinois: The American Botanist, 1988.

Fiorillo, Victor. "The Last Saffron Farmer." *Philadelphia Magazine* (December 2005): 213–214.

Fletcher, Stevenson Whitcomb. *Pennsylvania Agriculture and Country Life, 1640–1940,* 2 vols. Harrisburg, Pennsylvania: Pennsylvania Historical and Museum Commission, 1950.

Gettle, Jere and Emilee Gettle. *The Heirloom Life Gardener: The Baker Creek Way of Growing Your Own Food Easily and Naturally.* Mansfield, Missouri: Baker Creek Heirloom Seed Company, 2011.

Goldman, Amy. *The Compleat Squash: A Passionate Grower's Guide to Pumpkins, Squashes, and Gourds.* New York: Artisan Books, 2005.

Goldman, Amy. *The Heirloom Tomato: From Garden to Table.* New York, New York: Bloomsbury USA, 2003.

Goldman, Amy. *Melons for the Passionate Grower.* New York, New York: Artisan, 2002.

Gough, Robert and Cheryl Moore-Gough. *The Complete Guide to Saving Seeds.* North Adams, Massachusetts: Storey Publishing, 2011.

Green, Wesley. *Vegetable Gardening the Colonial Williamsburg Way: 18th Century Methods for Today's Organic Gardeners.* Emmaus, Pennsylvania: Rodale Press, 2012

Gundaker, Grey and Judith McWillie. *No Space Hidden. The Spirit of African American Yard Work.* Knoxville, Tennessee: University of Tennessee Press, 2005.

Gundaker, Grey, ed. *Keep Your Head to the Sky: Interpreting African American Home Ground.* Charlottesville, Virginia: University of Virginia Press, 1998.

Hatch, Peter J. *"A Rich Spot of Earth": Thomas Jefferson's Revolutionary Garden at Monticello.* New Haven, Connecticut: Yale University Press, 2012.

Hedrick, U. P. *A History of Horticulture in America to 1860.* N.Y.: Oxford University Press, 1950.

Heirloom Seed Project. *Year 2005 Catalog.* Lancaster, Pennsylvania: Landis Valley Museum, 2005.

Howell, Catherine H. *Flora Mirabilis: How Plants Have Shaped the World.* Washington, DC: The National Geographic Society, 2009.

Iannotti, Marie. *The Beginner's Guide to Growing Heirloom Vegetables.* Portland, Oregon: Timber Press, 2012.

Jellett, Edwin C. *Germantown Gardens and Gardeners,* Philadelphia, Pennsylvania: Horace F. McCann, 1914.

Jordan, Terry G. *German Seed in Texas Soil: Immigrant Farmers in Nineteenth Century Texas.* Austin, Texas: University of Texas Press, 1975.

Keene, Suzanne. "Pa. Farm Heritage Seed Program." *Lancaster Farming* (September 27, 1986), back page +.

Keyser, Alan G. "Gardens and Gardening Among the Pennsylvania Germans." *Pennsylvania Folklife.* XXI (Spring 1971): 2–15.

Klein, William M., Jr. *Gardens of Philadelphia and the Delaware Valley.* Philadelphia, Pennsylvania: Temple University Press, 1995.

Klimuska, Ed. "His Passion is Saving Old Seeds." *Lancaster New Era,* Lancaster, Pennsylvania (September 5, 1986): Back page +.

Lapp, Laura Ann. *An Amish Garden: A Year in the Life of an Amish Garden*: Intercourse, Pennsylvania: Good Books, 2013.

Lehoullier, Craig. "A Spectrum of Heirloom Tomatoes." *American Gardener* (March/April 2013): 34–38.

Leighton, Ann. *American Gardens of the Nineteenth Century: "For Comfort and Affluence."* Amherst, Massachusetts: University of Massachusetts Press, 1987.

Leighton, Ann. *Early American Gardens: "For Meat or Medicine."* Amherst, Massachusetts: University of Massachusetts Press, 1986.

Leighton, Ann. *American Gardens in the Eighteenth Century: "For Use or for Delight."* Amherst, Massachusetts: University of Massachusetts Press, 1986.

Male, Carolyn J. *100 Heirloom Tomatoes for the American Garden.* New York, NY: Workman Publishing, 1999.

Markham, Brett L. *Mini Farming: Self Sufficiency on 1/4 Acre.* New York, New York: Skyhorse Publishing, 2012

Marranca, Bonnie, Ed. *American Garden Writing: Gleanings from Garden Lives Then and Now.* New York: Penguin Books, 1988.

Martins, Tovah. *Heirloom Flowers: Vintage Flowers for Modern Gardens.* New York: Fireside, 1999.

Michel, Carol. "Graft is Good." *Pennsylvania Gardener* (July/August, 2013) 44–45.

Millspaugh, Charles F. *American Medicinal Plants.* Reprint, New York: Dover Publications, 1974.

Morris, Alex. "What Can't Kale Do?" *New York Magazine* (July 29-August 5, 2013): 7–8.

Morris, Julia Lewis, comp. *From Seed to Flower, Philadelphia 1681–1876: A Horticultural Point of View.* Philadelphia, Pennsylvania: The Pennsylvania Horticultural Society 1976.

Morse, Alice Earle. *Old Time Gardens: Newly set forth.* New York: The Macmillan Company, 1901.

Nabhan, Gary Paul. *Enduring Seeds: Native American Agriculture and Wild Plant Conservation.* Tucson, Arizona: University of Arizona Press, 2002.

Pape, Christine, ed. *Always Growing: The Story of the Morris Arboretum.* Philadelphia, Pennsylvania: The Morris Arboretum, 2010.

Pollan, Michael. "Opium Made Easy," *Harpers Magazine* (April 1, 1997): 1–7.

Ray, Janisse. *The Seed Underground: A Growing Revolution to Save Food.* White River Junction, New Hampshire: Chelsea Green Publishing, 2012.

Richman, Irwin. *Pennsylvania German Farms, Gardens, and Seeds: Landis Valley in Four Centuries.* Atglen, Pennsylvania: Schiffer Publishing. 2007.

Richman, Irwin. "The Pennsylvania-German Four Square Garden". *The Magazine Antiques* (July 2001): 92–97.

Richman, Irwin. *Seed Art: The Package Made Me Buy It.* Atglen, Pennsylvania: Schiffer Publishing, 2008.

Riotte, Louise. *Carrots Love Tomatoes and Roses Love Garlic: Secrets of Companion Planting for Successful Gardening.* North Adams, Massachusetts: Storey Publishing, 1998.

Rogers, Marc. *Saving Seeds: The Gardener's Guide to Growing and Storing Vegetable and Flower Seeds.* North Adams, Massachusetts: Storey Publishing, 1990.

Sills, Vaughan. *Places for the Spirit: Traditional African American Gardens.* San Antonio, Texas: Trinity University Press, 2010.

Spencer, Darrell. *The Gardens of Salem: The Landscape History of a Moravian Town in North Carolina.* Winston–Salem, North Carolina: Old Salem, Inc., 1997.

Staff of the Liberty Hyde Bailey Hortorium. *Hortus Third: A Concise Dictionary of Plants Cultivated in the United States and Canada.* New York & London: Macmillan Publishing Company, 1976.

Stoltzfus, Lee J. "Elements of a Four-Square Garden" *Kitchen Garden Magazine* (Dec 1996/Jan 1997): 20–23.

Strickland, Sue. *Heirloom Vegetables: A Home Gardener's Guide to Finding and Growing Vegetables From the Past.* New York: Fireside, 1998.

Thompson, Ann Newlin, et al. *Germantown Green: a Living Legacy of Gardens Orchards, and Pleasure Grounds.* Philadelphia, Pennsylvania: The Wyck Association, The Germantown Historical Society, The Maxwell Mansion, 1982.

Turner, Carole B. *Seed Sowing and Saving.* North Andover, Massachusetts: Storey Publishing, 1997.

Weaver, William Woys. *As American as Apple Pie: The Foodlore and Fakelore of Pennsylvania Dutch Cuisine.* Philadelphia, Pennsylvania: University of Pennsylvania Press, 2013.

Weaver, William Woys. *Sauer's Herbal Cures: America's First Book of Botanic Healing, 1762–1778.* New York and London: Routledge, 2001.

Weaver, William Woys. *Heirloom Vegetable Gardening: A Master Gardeners Guide to Planting, Seed Saving and Cultural History.* New York: Holt, 1997.

Welch, William C. and Greg Grant. *Heirloom Gardening in the South: Yesterday's Plants for Today's Gardens.* College Station, Texas: Texas A & M University Press, 2011

Westlake, Ton. "The Hudson Valley Seed Library Now Growing from Seed to Farm Stand at Hollengold Farms: *Country Wisdom News* (August 2013): 1+

Westmacott, Richard. *African American Gardens: Yards in Rural South.* Nashville, Tennessee: University of Tennessee Press, 1992.

Whealy, Diane Ott. *Gathering: Memoir of a Seed Saver.* Decorah Iowa: Seed Savers Exchange, 2011.

Wiser, Vivian, ed. *Two Centuries of American Agriculture.* Washington, DC: Agricultural History Society, 1976.

Withee, John E. *Growing and Cooking Beans.* Dublin, New Hampshire: Yankee Publishing, Inc., 1980.

Wood, Rudolph, ed. *The Pennsylvania Germans.* Princeton, New Jersey: Princeton University Press, 1942.

Wulf, Andrea. *The Brother Gardeners: A Generation of Gentlemen Naturalists and the Birth of an Obsession.* New York, New York: Vintage, 2010.

Wulf, Andrea. *The Founding Gardeners: The Revolutionary Generation, Nature and the Shaping of the American Nation.* New York, New York: Vintage, 2012.

INDEX

African-American gardens, 29
Agrimony, 228
Amaranth, 250
Amaranthus, 266
Amaryllis, 236
Ambridge, PA, 155
Amish, 46, 49, 158-159, 195
Angelica, 250
Anglo-Dutch gardens, 34-41
Antes, Henry, 119
Arizona, 27
Arums, 250
Asparagus, 238
Aster, 250
Aster, New England, 27
Bachelor's Button, 251
Balsam Apple, 238
Barger, John, 107
Barre, Anette, 21
Bartram, John, 166, 170-172, 184
Bartram's Gardens, 172-174
Basil, 228, 251
Germantown, Battle of, 110
Baum, Walter Emerson, 45
Beanhole, 11
Beans, 23, 202, 214-217, 239-240
Bears Breeches, 252
Becker, Emma, 64
Beets, 202, 220, 241
Bernville, PA, 27
Beiler, Joseph F., 49
Beiler, Sadie Smucker, 49
Beissel, Conrad, 115
Bennett Bobb Log House, 110-111
Berks County, PA, 163
Bethabara Hortus Medicus, 152
Bethlehem, PA, 89, 136-141
Birney, William Verplank, 12
Black-eyed Susan, 27
Blackberry Lily, 232, 252
Blatt, C. G., 20
Bleeding Heart, 252
B, K. Bliss and Sons, 191
Blue Hills at Stone Barns, 9
Bloodroot, 252
Bowman's Hill Wildflower Preserve, 181
Brendle, Thomas R., 49, 60
Brubaker, Daniel, 197
Burnet, 228, 252
Burnside Plantation, 139-140
Butterfly Weed, 232-233
Burpee, W. Atlee, 194
Cabbage, 78-79, 88, 226-241
Cactus, 32
Calendula, 233, 253
Callaway Gardens, 39
California, 26-30
Calla lilies, 29
Camomile, 230, 253
Caraway, 228
Carrots, 202, 220
Carter's Grove Plantation, 88
Cassidy, Gerald, 30
Castor Bean, 253

Celeriac, 241
Celery, 241
Celosia, 233
Cemeteries, 126-128
Champlain, Samuel de, 23
Chard, Swiss, 202, 247
Charming Forge, 54
Chas. C. Hart Seed Co., 266
Chelsea Physic Garden, 177
Chromolthography, 191, 193
Child, Julia, 83
Chili peppers, 31
Chives, 228, 253
Christ Lutheran Church, 126-127
Cilantro, 230
Cleome, 254
Christmas Rose, 74
Church Town, PA, 36
Clemens, Hanna Rittenhouse, 55
Cockscomb, 233
Coffin, Marian, 182
Collards, 220
Columbine, 233
Comfrey, 228
Coneflower, 235
Colonial Pennsylvania Plantation, 176
Colonial Williamsburg, 173-174
Cold frames, 90
Compton, 179
Corn, 23, 222-123, 242
Conrad Weiser Homestead, 166-67
Cooper, Colin Campbell, 30
Copeland, Pamela, 182
Coriander, 230
Cosmos, 254
Cotton, 254
Crocus, 254
Cucumbers, 202, 223-124, 242
Daffodils, 255
Dame's Rocket, 255
David Landreth and Sons, 188, 191
Landreth, See David Landreth and
    Sons
Deer, 53
DeTurk House, 161
Die Lott, 55
Dill, 230, 255
Diller, George, 264
duPont, Éleuthère Irénée, 43-44
duPont, Victorine, 93
Dunkelberger, Ralph D., 89
Doughnuts, 55
Easter, 20, 97
Elephant Ears, 236
Elcampane, 233
Endive, 242
English style garden, 109
Ephrata Cloister, 115-116
Ephrata, PA, 115
Falkner Swamp Church, 128
Fennel, 228
Fernery, 180
Ferry, David Morse, 193
Feverfew, 233

Fisher House, 10
Flax, 255
Floracroft Seed Garden, 190
Florida, 26-27
Flowerpots, 265
Flushing, NY, 69
Forget-me-not, 256
Foodshed, 9
Francis, Richard, 189
Franciscans, 28
Franz, John, 49
Frederick, MD, 123
French vegetable gardens, 43-45
Frogmore Kitchen Garden, 39
Frontier Culture Museum of Virginia,
    107-109
Frosese, Lyle, 11
Chives, Garlic, 228
Garden boards, 65
Garden implements, 58
Gemberling-Rex House, 105
General Horatio Gates House, 117-118
George Whythe garden, 38
Geraniums, 14
Germantown, PA, 129-136
Germany, gardens in, 45-48
Gherkin, 223
Gilbert, Conrad, 97
Ginger, American, 256
Gladioli, 56, 256
Glen Rock, PA, 264
Golden Plough Tavern, 117-118
Gourds, 121, 202, 225-226, 242
Grain Cradle, 123
Great Valley, 85-86, 159
Greenhouse, 135
Grider, Rufus, 142
Ground Cherry, 212
Grumblethorpe, 130, 134
Haidt, Johann Valentine, 142
Haines, Caspar Wistar, 67, 69
Haines, Hannah M., 67, 69, 189
Haines, Jane Bowne, 67, 69-70,
    131-132
Haines, Margaret Wistar, 69
Haines, Reuben, 67-71, 131
Halloway, Mark, 153
Hameau de la Reine, 43
Harmonists, 93, 95-96, 154-157
Harmonie, 154-155
Harmony Museum, 157
Harmony, PA, 157
Harmony Society, 153-157
Hans Herr House, 83-84
Hatch, Peter, 184
Hedrick, U. P., 23
Heebner, Susanna, 110
Heirloom Seed Project, 197-235
Heller, Lizzie, 65
Hensler, Maximillian, 189
Henry Antes Plantation, 119-121
Herb and Garden Faire, 198, 200, 204
Herr, Christian and Hannah, 113
Hialeah, FL, 26

Bethabara Park, Historic, 152
Historic Bethabara Park, 152
Historic Rittenhouse Town, 133
Rittenhouse Town, Historic , 133
Historic Schaefferstown, 105-106
Schaefferstown, Historic, 105-106
Hockessin, DE, 182
Hollyhock, 234, 256
Honeybees, 37
Hops, 59
Horehound, 230, 256
Horseradish, 257
Hyacinth, 257
Hortus Botanica, Leiden, 41
House Plants, 264
Huis ten Bosch, 41
Hummel farm, 57
Hyacinth, 257
Hyacinth Bean, 234, 257
Ingham, Charles C., 14
Iris, 257
Impatiens, 257
Iroquois, 23
Irrigation, 48
Jacob's Cattle Beans, 11
Jasper, Margaret, 33
Jefferson, Thomas, 184
Jerusalem artichokes, 25
Jesuits, 27, 288
Job's Tears, 234, 258
Johannes Mueller House, 148
Johnson and Stokes, 190
Johnstown, PA, 125
Johnstown Flood, 125
Lamb's Ear, 258
Larkspur, 234, 258
Leenswaart, Beth, 200
Lemon Balm, 258
Lilies, 258
Lily of the Valley, 258
Lobelia, 259
Lovage, 230, 259
Lunaria, 234
Lungwort, 259
Lupine, 258
Kale, 219, 243
Keen, Robert Martin, 55
Keim House, 10
Kelly Farm, 57
Keyser, Alan G., 49, 60, 64-65
Kin, Mathias, 129
Kohlrabi, 243
Kraus Studios, 22
Kuhn, Adam Dr., 177
Landis, Elizabeth, 52-53
Landis, Emma, 73
Landis, George D., 73
Landis, Henry H., 73
Landis, Henry K., 57, 73
Landis, Jacob, 51-52
Landis Valley Mennonite Church
    Cemetery, 128
Landis Valley Village and Farm
    Museum, 11, 73-83, 101-103

Las Cruces, NM, 32
Lebanon County, PA, 162
Lee, Jonathan, 65
Lee, Maria, 65
Leeks, 220, 243
Lettuce, 9, 202, 217-243
Lititz, PA, 89, 143-149
Lititz Historical Museum, 148
Lititz Springs Park, 143, 145-146
Lima Beans, 215.24
Locavore, 9
Logan, James, 134
Luck, David E, 49, 60
McClure, Pearl, 21
Mangelwurzel, 243
Lily, Madonna, 236
Maple sugar, 25
Marjoram, 230
Markert, Herman, 57, 127
Marshall, Christopher, 69
Meehan, Thomas, 129, 168-169
Melons, 202, 224, 294
Meng, Melchior, 129
Mennonites, 9, 11, 45, 59, 115, 129-133, 195
Mennonite Historical Society, 83
Mexico, 23
Millbach, PA, 162
Miller, Charlie, 65
Miller, Steven S., 197-199
Mints, 232, 258
Mission Inn, 27
Millan, Hans, 67
Mr. Carson's Vegetable Garden, 39
Moleplant, 230, 259
Monarda, 260
Montgomery County, PA, 84, 110
Monticello, 184
Moravian Historical Society, 142
Moravian Museum of Bethlehem, Inc., 137
Moravians, 89-93, 119, 136-152
Morning Glory, 260
Mosteller Wild Goose bean, 217, 239
Mullein, 260
Mushrooms, 25
Morris Arboretum, 179-180
Morris, John T., 179
Morris, Lydia T., 179
Mt Cuba Center, 182-183
Nasturtium, 260
Native Americans, 23-25, 27, 107, 195
Nazareth, PA, 89, 142
Nemours, 43-44
New Hope, PA, 181
New Mexico, 27, 30, 32
Newtown Square, PA, 176
North Adams, MA, 21
Nuttall, Thomas, 130
Oak Park, IL, 21
Obedient Plant, 260
Oenothera, 253, 260
Palace of the Governors (NM), 30
Old Economy Village, 154-156
Old Salem Museums and Gardens, 150-151

Oley Valley, 160-161
Olmstead Brothers, 166
Onions, 221, 244
Open pollination, 201
Opium, 191
Orach, 202
Owens, Chris, 133
Palatinate, 107
Parsnip, 202
Pansy, 261
Parsley, 231, 261
Pastorius, Daniel Francis, 129
Patriotic Order Sons of America, 105
Peale, James, 15
Peale, Raphaelle, 14, 15
Peas, 81, 217-218, 245
Perkiomenville, PA, 119
Penn, William, 22, 175
Penn, Admiral Sir William, 33
Pennsbury Manor, 37, 175
Pennsylvania German garden plants, 61, 63
Pennsylvania German gardens, 45-98, 101-169
Pennsylvania Hospital Physic Garden, 177-178
Pennypacker Mills, 168-169
Pennypacker, Samuel W., 168-169
Pennyroyal, 228
Peony, 261
Peru, 23
Pesticides, 59
Peter Wentz Farmstead, 110-112
Philadelphia, PA, 129-135, 170-172, 177-180
Phillipsburg Manor, 40
Pigpens, 59, 76
Pinks, 262
Pippert, Nancy, 198
Plimouth Plantation, 36
Plowing, 20
Phlox, 261
Pocantico Hills, NY, 9
Ponce de Leon Hotel, 34
Popcorn, 222
Poppy, 260
Potager, 43-44
Potatoes, 245
Pratt family, 176
Prince Nursery, 69
Pumpkins, 246
Quakers, 67, 70, 129-135, 176, 189, 194
Quiet Valley Living Historical Farm, 122-125
Rabbit hutches, 59
Radishes, 246
Raised bed gardens, 45-83, 101-156
Raised bed garden plan, 54
Rapp, George, 96
Reichenau, Germany, 45
Renfrew Museum and Garden, 104
Rhubarb, 246
Rittenhouse Town, 133-134
Riverside, CA, 27
Rockefeller, Mr. and Mrs. John D.,

Jr., 40
Rogueing, 201
Rose Campion, 235, 262
Rosemary, 74, 231
Rote Studios, 22
Rototiller, 59
Royer, David, 104
Rue, 262
Runway gardens, 92-95, 96
Rutabagas, 202, 221
Rye, 246
Safflower, 235, 262
Saffron, 55
Sage, 230, 262
Salem, NC, 89
Salsify, 222, 247
St. Augustine, FL, 26
Saint Gaul, Switzerland, 45
San Gabriel Mission, 28
Santa Barbara Mission, 28
Saxe-Weimer, Duke of, 153
Schaeffer, Alexander, 105
Schaefferstown, PA, 105
Schifferstadt Architectural Museum, 123-124
Schultz, Melchior, 110
Schwartzbeeren, 261
Schwenkfelders, 45, 110
Schwenksville, PA, 168
Seed bags, 186
Seed Savers Exchange, 13, 196-197, 199
Seed saving techniques, 205, 208-209, 211, 213
Seed storage, 208
Senecas, 23
Shakers, 190-191
Shikellamy, Chief, 167
Slavery, 29
Snake plant, 14
Snyder, Sallie, 64
Sorrel, 247
South Carolina, 23
Southernwood, 262
Spanish, 26-32
Spinach, 202, 219
Squash, 224, 247
Sprecher's Sons, 19
Springfield, MO, 11
Staunton, VA, 107
Stouchsburg, PA, 126, 163-165
Stroudsburg, PA, 122
Steigerwalt, The Reverend E. O., 45
Steigerwalt, Florence C., 53
Stenton, 134-135
Stoltzfus, Lee, 11, 66, 68, 196-198
Strickland, William, 67, 131
Strickland, Sue, 187
Stuckey Family, 21
Superstitions, 61-63
Sunflower, 262
Sweet Cicely, 230
Sweet Potato, 226, 247
Sweet William, 236
Tansy, 263
Tea, mint, 98, 258

Texas, 27
Thanksgiving, 20
Thomas, Guy, 13
Thomas E. Brendle Museum, 105
Thyme, 55, 127-128, 231
Tillers, mechanical, 86
Tithonia, 263
Tobacco, 24
Tomatoes, 9, 210-213, 248-249
Topiary, 83, 165
Tree Peony, 264
Tulips, 263
Turnips, 202, 221, 250
Upper Canada Village, 20
Valerian, 263
Van Cortlandt Manor, 41
Vermont Bean Seed Company, 13
Vernon Park, 129
Veronica, 264
Versailles, 42-43
Vineland, Ontario, 9
Von Mahfeld, Joseph Molitar, 46
Von Schweinitz, Louis David, 93, 170
Von Zinzindorf, Count Nikolaus Ludwig, 69, 119
Wagner-Ritter House and Garden, 125-126
Onion, Walking, 230, 244
Warner, Ralph, 11
Washington, George, 110
Washington Crossing State Park, 181
Watermelon, 224, 250
Fencing, wattle, 38
Waynesboro, PA, 104
Weaver, William Woys, 49, 83, 199
Weier, Frank, 9, 11
Weiser, Conrad, 166-167
Whealy, Diane and Kent, 195
Whitfield, George, 119, 142
Whitfield House, 142
William III and Mary?, 33
Williamsburg, VA, 38, 40, 51, 173
Willow Street, PA, 113
Winston-Salem, NC, 150-152·
Wissahickon Creek, 179
Wistar, Dr. Caspar, 130
Wister, John, 130
Wister, John Caspar, 134
Wister, Owen, 130
Wisteria, 130
Withee, John E., 11, 13
Wood, Grant, 14, 18
Worcester, PA, 110
Womelsdorf, PA, 116
Wyck, 67-72, 131-132, 134
Yarrow, 235, 264
York Agricultural and Industrial Museum, 117-118
York, PA, 110-111
Zepper, Johann, 122